Hamlyn

Eleanor Hughes

Silver for Collectors

illustrated by Peter Henville

Hamlyn · London

FOREWORD

It is a daunting task to cover some six centuries of silversmiths' work in a relatively small book and inevitably this must be just a short introduction to the subject. However I hope the reader will get a glimpse of the enormous scope and variety of the craft.

In the past, a storeroom full of silver represented both a healthy bank balance (to be melted down in times of financial difficulty) and a status symbol. But silver is not only valuable and beautiful, it is also useful, and a whole range of items was made in the precious metal, from the most humble – teaspoons, porringers and saucepans – to the most lavish – presentation cups, toilet and dinner services, etc.

Through the centuries silversmiths have devised numerous ways in which to work and decorate their metal – hammering, punching, cutting, moulding and engraving. The story of how the different styles and modes of working evolved in all the major European countries, to be adopted in different ways throughout the rest of the continent and ultimately throughout the world, is the subject of this book.

Eleanor Hughes

Published by The Hamlyn Publishing Group Limited
London · New York · Sydney · Toronto
Astronaut House, Feltham, Middlesex, England

© Copyright The Hamlyn Publishing Group Limited 1974

ISBN 0 600 38060 2
Phototypeset by Filmtype Services Limited, Scarborough, England
Colour separations by Colour Workshop, England
Printed by Mateu Cromo, Spain

CONTENTS

INTRODUCTION

The intrinsic value of silver is of secondary importance to the form into which it is made. From earliest times man has fashioned this precious metal for various purposes, either to adorn his person, to complement his mode of living, or to express his reverence for divine or worldly powers.

The qualities of silver are its brightness, power of reflection, malleability and durability. The durability no doubt has contributed to its preservation, unlike many more fragile materials. On the other hand pure silver is too soft for working purposes and for this reason it is combined with other harder metals, usually copper. This process is known as alloying. The amount of alloy allowed has been rigidly controlled in England since 1238, when an Act of Parliament was passed decreeing that the silver used could not be less pure than that employed for coinage. In England in 1526–27 the Troy weight was substituted for the old Tower pound and is still in use today. The Troy ounce is divided into pennyweights: 20dwt equals 1oz.

The standard of silver is as follows. 11oz 2dwt of pure silver is combined with 18dwt of alloy in every 12oz gross. In modern terms this is referred to as ·925. The standard has not altered throughout the years with the exception of a short period between 1697 and 1720, when the amount of alloy allowed was decreased to 10dwt to prevent the clipping and melting of coins, two offences practised to try and meet the demands for large quantities of plate ordered after the restoration of the monarchy in 1660. This is known as the Britannia standard. In Europe the amount of alloy varies in the different countries, and in many cases the standard is lower than that allowed in England. Here it is forbidden to offer for sale silver of foreign origin below standard and less than a hundred years old.

The only slight drawback of silver is the tarnishing which occurs, caused by the metal combining with sulphur or chlorides. However this does have one advantage as repairs, patches and the removal of engraving and other decoration are more easily detected on tarnished pieces.

Putti making silver beakers. Four copperplate engravings, Augsburg, early 18th century

In Augspurg bey Moritz Mittrach.

Methods of decoration

Engraving

Engraving, one of the most common methods of decoration, is achieved by the removal of surface metal with a sharp tool. By varying the amount of pressure shading effects can be produced; areas can also be hatched or matted to achieve the same effect. Matting is attained by repeatedly striking the surface with a punch engraved with a cluster of small circles.

The 17th-century engravings executed by Dutch and German silversmiths illustrate some of the most outstanding examples of this work in existence. The medallion reproduced is by Simon de Passe. Born in Cologne in about 1590, he worked in Utrecht from 1612 to 1615, moved to London in 1615 and to Paris in 1623. After a short stay in Utrecht he settled in Copenhagen, where he died in 1647. Among noteworthy pieces attributed to him are a set of plaques inset in a table in the Rosenborg Palace, Copenhagen, and all but one are after prints by his father, to whom he was apprenticed.

Knife and fork. Dutch, early 17th century

above Spice box, about 1685; *below* Spice box. Silver-gilt. About 1685; *right* Medallion by Simon de Passe. Silver-gilt. 1615–22

The medallion, signed S.P. and presumably executed during his stay in England, depicts portraits of James I, his wife Anne of Denmark and their son Charles, Prince of Wales, and on the reverse their arms and devices. A number of other portrait medallions by de Passe are in the British Museum, London.

The knife and fork illustrated are examples of Dutch craftsmanship, and are unmarked. The scenes depicted on the handles are taken from the New Testament and the openwork terminals are decorated on a niello ground (see p. 12) with formal ornament centred by emblems of marriage.

The English spice box dates from the second half of the 17th century. According to John F. Hayward, this engraving appears to be of local origin, unlike many earlier designs found on English silver which can be traced to foreign pattern books. If one reviews the pieces recorded dating from this period the similarity of technique but variation of designs suggests a certain spontaneity in the engraver.

Engraving of cartouches centred by armorials, initials or

7

inscriptions adds interest and value to a piece, provided it is contemporary. The following are some examples of the more usual designs used for cartouches from the middle of the 17th century to the first part of the 19th.

The cartouche of 1673 is taken from a Charles II dish, illustrating simple crossed plumes. In the early 18th century, through French influence, more elaborate examples were produced. The first, although somewhat restrained, displays formal scrollwork, foliage and husks, headed by a shell. The next example which appears on a salver of 1733 is more elaborate; the armorials are surrounded by brickwork, bordered by symmetrical scrolls and foliage incorporating a shepherd and shepherdess, vases of flowers, and at the base male demi-figures flanking a mythological scene.

Unfortunately, most engravers are anonymous, as this type of work was rarely signed. One we do know of is Benjamin Rhodes, who worked for the banker-goldsmith Sir Richard Hoare, from 1st January 1694 to 6th January 1698, and whose account book is in the possession of Hoare's bank. Although his work is unsigned, various pieces have been identified from entries and sketches in the book. One example is a cup and cover by John Bodington, London, 1697, made for Trinity College, Cambridge. From the *Catalogue of Engravers*, compiled by Horace Walpole, we also know that another master, Simon Gribelin of Blois, arrived in this country in about 1680 and published *A book of ornament useful to Jewellers, watchmakers and all other Artists*. One of his most important known works is a salver made for Charles Montague, Earl of Halifax, in about 1695, now in the Burrell Collection, Glasgow.

The next cartouche represents the style used in the second quarter of the 18th century during the Rococo period, showing an asymmetrical design. The cartouche of 1780 is typical of the Adam era, displaying husks pendent from *paterae* and ribbon ties. The last example is frequently seen on work by Paul Storr and other Regency silversmiths. The escutcheon is bordered by formal scrolls and headed by a foliate mantling.

Six examples of engraving on cartouches from the 17th to the 19th century: *a* late 17th century; *b* about 1700; *c* about 1730; *d* Rococo style, about 1745; *e* about 1780; *f* about 1810

a

b

c

d

e

f

Chasing and embossing

Chasing is a method of decorating the surface where the metal is indented with a mallet or chisel. No material is removed and the pattern is visible on the reverse. When produced in low relief, it is described as flat chasing. It is also used to improve the sharpness of castings. Embossing or repoussé work also falls into this category, the difference being that the effect is produced by working from the back to achieve a pattern in high relief.

The plaque illustrated is taken from a pair of 17th-century Dutch wall sconces, signed and dated 1622, by Adam van Vianen of Utrecht. The scene depicts Diana and Actaeon. The detail and quality of the work has seldom been surpassed. The feeling of depth is achieved by the lifelike modelling of the figures and the exquisite detail of the landscape, in both the foreground and the background. The second illustration, of a unicorn embossed in high relief, decorates the lid of a Charles II tankard of 1680.

Casting

Casting is used when several items of the same shape are required, such as the spouts of teapots, finials, scroll brackets, handles and thumbpieces. Cast straps were often used when mounting other materials, for example rare porcelain, stoneware and various shells. Sometimes whole pieces are made in this way. Wax casting is one method employed to produce this type of work. This is achieved by immersing a wax model in moulding sand and when the hot liquid is poured into the mould the wax melts or vaporizes, and as the metal solidifies it takes its place. If a hollow casting is required the wax model is centred by a clay core which can later be removed.

The jug, made in London in 1720, is an example of this type of work. The body, modelled as a snail's shell, has a mask applied at the lip and is supported by a dragon couchant on a spreading oval base. The handle is in the form of a sea serpent gripping the waved rim between its jaws. Work produced in this way is normally much heavier than a piece which has been raised.

Niello

Niello decoration is a form of enamelling where the surface is incised, applied with an alloy of silver, lead, copper and sulphur, fired and finally filed level and polished. The box illustrated is of Russian origin, made in Vologda in 1845. The view on the lid is of the Nevski Prospect of St Petersburg. From the 17th century onwards, Russian craftsmen continued to produce niellowork, which is frequently combined with gilding when the result is most attractive.

Gilding

Gilding today is done by electrolysis. This somehow lacks the deep rich colour of fire gilding, the method employed before electrogilding was invented in 1805 by Brugnatelli. The technique of fire gilding involved a solution of gold and mercury, which when heated gave off poisonous fumes and is therefore seldom used today.

To determine whether gilding is contemporary can be difficult. The areas gilded are sometimes a good indication. For example, at certain periods parcel-gilding (gilding specific

Silver-gilt and niello snuff box. Russian, Vologda 1845

George III sweetmeat
basket by Peter and
Jonathan Bateman.
London 1790

areas) was in favour as opposed to covering the whole surface,
with the exception of the underside of the base, which was
frequently left plain before the introduction of electrolysis. In
Holland during the 17th and 18th centuries, the use of gilding
was the exception rather than the rule, whereas the reverse is
true in Germany, except during the second half of the 18th
century. Another indication is the chipping of small particles
seen on fire gilding caused by wear, unlike electrogilding
which gradually fades and disappears.

Piercing

Piercing became popular in England during the 18th century,
and is associated with baskets used for many purposes. The
earlier examples were of heavy gauge and the piercing was
carried out with a saw. These pieces are accompanied by chased
decoration, applied cast borders and similar bases. By the

William and
Mary teapot,
London 1689

middle of the century silversmiths were beginning to use
factory-made sections, combining various patterns. Although
the whole effect was attractive, the end result was an article
of a rather light and flimsy nature. The basket illustrated is in
the Adam style and incorporates bright-cut engraving, so-
called because the metal is cut to produce varying degrees of
reflection.

Applied ornament

The William and Mary teapot, London, 1689, is a good example
of English cut-card work. Various patterns were cut out of
sheets of silver and applied to surfaces to produce this form of
embellishment, which is normally found at handle sockets,
spouts and on covers. In England the application was not
decorated, unlike the cut-card work of Dutch origin which is
frequently engraved.

The ornament is a forerunner of the applied strapwork
brought to England by the Huguenots, which became very
popular in the early 18th century. The leaf-like straps found

encircling the lower half of vessels later developed into cast straps incorporating guilloche ornament, husks and shells. Others of a broader design were pierced and applied with marine motifs and masks. A matted background frequently accompanied this work.

Filigree ornament is composed of narrow strips of silver resembling wire, some plain, others twisted to produce a corded effect, intricately woven together. Again it is a form of applied decoration, but this time is not associated with English work. The beaker of Swedish origin, by Rudolf Wittkopf of Stockholm, 1698, has a silver-gilt background overlaid with a filigree sleeve composed of panels of floral designs within corded borders, repeated on the ball feet, cover and finial.

Filigree, usually unmarked, can be difficult to identify. It is a form of craftsmanship frequently undervalued when one considers the skill required to produce this type of work. During the second half of the 18th century apprentices in Friesland were obliged to submit an item demonstrating their ability in this field before they were admitted to the silversmiths' guild.

Beaker and cover by
Rudolf Wittkopf. Swedish.
Stockholm 1698

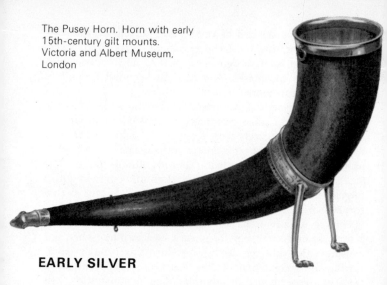

The Pusey Horn. Horn with early
15th-century gilt mounts.
Victoria and Albert Museum,
London

EARLY SILVER

Relatively few items have survived from the Gothic period,
dating approximately from the end of the 12th century to the
first quarter of the 16th century in England. With the exception
of spoons the majority of pieces still in existence are of ecclesiastical origin, for example chalices and patens, although some
items of domestic plate are found in church collections,
adopted after the Reformation on account of their secular
appearance which in many cases has contributed to their sur-
vival. Frequently domestic plate was melted down, not just to
provide currency, but to be refashioned. Other items which
escaped the melting pot are silver-mounted vessels – coconut
cups, drinking horns and mazers. Mazers are circular wooden
bowls, used for drinking, with applied silver lip bands, on
similar bases. During the destruction of vast quantities of plate
in the reign of Henry VIII, these pieces were probably considered of little significance on account of the relatively small
amount of silver involved in their construction. The Pusey
Horn comes in this category.

Drinking horns were in general use in Anglo-Saxon days,
but by the late Middle Ages they retained only prestige value.
This oxhorn is applied with a simple lip band. The tip is surmounted by a beast's head below a chased band of Gothic

leaves. The band encircling the body raised on paw feet is inscribed 'I King Knowde [Canute] give William Pewse [Pusey] this horn to hold by the hand'. The legend of the horn is that it was given, with Pusey Manor, Berkshire, by King Canute to one of his officers who penetrated a Saxon camp in disguise and warned the King of an impending attack.

The chalice of 1527, although dating from the end of this period, illustrates typical motifs found during the 15th century and earlier. The Lombardic lettering is a characteristic feature. The hexagonal stem rising from a balustrade with pinnacles at the angles displays panels of pierced quatrefoils within cabling, ornament found on contemporary architecture. It is interrupted by a compressed knop with lozenge-shaped facets embellished with masks.

The Renaissance

The influence of the Renaissance did not reach England until the early part of the 16th century, and then mainly through contact with German craftsmen. Henry VIII attracted many artists and goldsmiths to this country and also

Henry VIII chalice, London 1527

invested in large quantities of foreign plate. Another factor which led to the development of the Renaissance style was the circulation of pattern books issued by German, French, Italian and Dutch artists. Many elements can be identified, but the English craftsmen soon developed their own interpretation of the designs. When one takes into consideration the vast amount of plate produced, as recorded in contemporary inventories, a relatively small quantity has survived.

It appears that the skill of the English goldsmith frequently lacked the high standard achieved by his German counterpart, although some pieces display unquestionable ability. Among these is the Sutton Cup, of 1573, named after its maker, Isaac Sutton. This silver-gilt and rock crystal vessel illustrates many relevant features. The rock crystal bowl had a dual purpose at this date. As well as being decorative it was thought to cloud on contact with poison. The outline of the cup and the repoussé work on the foot and cover,

The Sutton Cup. An Elizabeth I cup and cover of silver-gilt and rock crystal, probably by Isaac Sutton. London 1573 displaying masks alternating with clusters of formalized fruit and stamped borders, are all features illustrating German influence. On the other hand the cartouches centred by ovolos at the lip and the engraving above, which does not appear on any other part of the mounts, are English characteristics.

In contrast, the livery pot is devoid of embellishment, with the exception of the stamped borders (the inscription around the body dates from the 17th century). The proportions of this vessel cannot be faulted, a characteristic which is most pleasing to the eye and so often lost with the addition of ornament of one kind or another. This piece is parcel-gilt, again an English feature.

Livery pots, used to replenish smaller vessels, were made for secular purposes. By the middle of the 17th century they were known as flagons and had acquired a cylindrical shape, resembling tankards, but of greater size. The majority which have survived from the early period are embellished with flat chasing in German style.

One of a pair of livery pots.
Parcel-gilt. London 1591

The Deane Tazza, probably by Robert Danbe. Parcel-gilt. London 1551

Another vessel of secular origin, which was in a church collection until it was sold in 1971, is the Deane Tazza.

The word tazza, meaning cup, has been adopted to describe vessels which are similar in outline to the font-shaped cups of the Gothic period, but display a more shallow bowl. The appealing inscription at the lip 'GIVE GOD THAKES [sic] FOR ALL THYNGS' is on a wrigglework ground. Wrigglework, as the term implies, is achieved by rocking the engraving tool from side to side thus producing a zigzag effect. It is sometimes found embellishing strapwork at this period.

The salt was considered the most important article of plate in the Middle Ages. Two early English salts in the form of figures, dating from the end of the 15th century, are the Huntsman's Salt at All Souls College and the Monkey Salt at New College, both in Oxford.

On the continent ship-shaped vessels, known as nefs, were considered equally important. They were originally used for drinking, but at a later date some were converted to votive vessels and presented to churches; others were fitted with salt cellars in the poop. An example of the latter is the Burghley Nef, made in Paris in 1482–83 by Pierre Le Flamand. It is now in the Victoria and Albert Museum and is one of the most important examples of French silver in England.

About the middle of the 16th century a new form was introduced, the standing salt, of circular or square outline, the base expanding below and the lip above. The domed covers were surmounted by the usual type of finials of vase, figure or baluster form. The decoration was typical of the period, elaborate embossed ornament with stamped borders. Small versions of these salts were produced and are very charming. The bell-shaped salt illustrated, maker's mark T.S., London, 1600, was a design used for a comparatively short period, dating from the last decade of the 16th century to the first quarter of the following century. This piece, resting on ball feet, is in three sections, the two lower for salt and the upper compartment pierced as a pepper caster. The relatively simple

Elizabeth I bell-shaped salt. Silver-gilt. London 1600

decoration displays strapwork and leaves on a matted ground. Gradually the salt diminished in size and at the end of the 17th century reached the proportions we are familiar with today.

The Magdalen cup derives its name from the fact that similar beakers appear in contemporary paintings in which Mary Magdalen is represented holding a pot of ointment resembling this vessel. Tracing the history of the beaker, an imported utensil associated with Scandinavia and the Low Countries, and used for ecclesiastical and secular purposes, has been complicated by the fact that in early inventories they were described by many different terms depending on their use at the time. Today the term beaker is used when referring to any vessel without handles, sometimes found with moulding

Elizabeth I Magdalen cup and cover. Silver-gilt. London 1573

Tigerware jug with Elizabeth I silver-gilt mounts. London about 1550

at the base, raised on a low foot or feet, with or without a cover.

The decoration on the Magdalen cup here displays many characteristics already mentioned when discussing the Sutton Cup (p. 18), but the engraving is the outstanding feature of this piece: a running foliate band appears at the lip above an applied girdle and below drapery festoons, pendent from canopies supporting birds and fruit swags.

The tigerware jug illustrated, a heavy earthenware vessel of baluster outline, with a handle well below the lip, derives its name from the mottled appearance of the pottery, and was imported from Germany. (The colour of the pottery is usually reddish brown but it can vary considerably.) The earlier examples have narrow lip mounts, usually engraved, and the hinge of the cover stands away from the body, forming a right angle with the handle. In later years this area was filled in, forming a box-like section. Gradually the jugs became taller; embossing replaced engraving and embellished the lip mount, cover and base. The jug illustrated is decorated at the

lip with engraved foliage, and a serrated border appears above the stamped foot mount. The cover is embossed with lobes, centred by a pear-shaped finial and fitted with an unusual thumbpiece composed of two entwined twigs, bearing fruit.

The Renaissance in Europe

The silver-gilt Monatsbecher, made in Augsburg, illustrates German craftsmanship at the end of the 16th century. Although it is somewhat restrained in design compared with the highly decorative work produced by the German Mannerist goldsmiths, the quality of the decoration is of a high standard. These beakers were originally made in sets of twelve, one for each month. Today it is rare to find more than two belonging to a set. The beaker is finely chased at the rim above an applied girdle with a frieze depicting a farmyard scene for the month of November. The base is embossed and chased with masks and scroll ornament on a stippled ground. Beakers of similar shape were decorated in a variety of ways. Some are engraved with Biblical or mythological scenes, while others depict hunting views. Frequently the decoration is found below the girdle, but a feature which seldom altered is the ornament on the base.

The Dutch drinking vessel in the form of a cock, realistically tooled, with detachable head, although slightly later in date, illustrates a foot of comparable design. Again the bearded masks appear on a stippled ground, but this time they are interspersed between scenes depicting birds in rustic landscapes.

During the 16th and 17th centuries in Germany and Switzerland, cups in the form of animals of all kinds, for example stags, bears, goats and squirrels, were in vogue. The majority of these were guild cups, the animal being the emblem of the guild. A most attractive example in the form of an owl with coconut body, realistically tooled silver feathers, feet and crowned detachable head, made in Germany during the early part of the 17th century, is in the Wernher Collection, Luton Hoo.

above Standing cup in the form of a cock. Silver-gilt. Dutch, Dordrecht 1608; *below* Monatsbecher. Silver-gilt. German, Augsburg about 1580

THE LOBATE STYLE

At the beginning of the 17th century in Holland another innovation occurred, known as the lobate or auricular (ear-like) style. It appears to be the only form of decoration that was 'invented' by the silversmiths and it found its fullest expression in this craft. It is a striking contrast to the formal ornament that had prevailed during the Renaissance period. The forms that were employed, such as dolphins, human figures (some of grotesque proportions), and marine motifs, were integrated with lobate or auricular mouldings. The whole produced a fluid effect so that on examination the eye moves from one area to another, each time interpreting new designs.

The van Vianen brothers were responsible for its invention and development. Paul spent most of his life outside Holland. He worked in Munich for the Duke of Bavaria, in Salzburg, and in 1601 moved to Prague, where he became *Kammergold-schmied* to Rudolf II, and died there in 1613. Adam on the other hand remained in Utrecht. One of his early pieces in the lobate manner is a tazza in the Victoria and Albert Museum, signed A.V. in monogram with Utrecht hallmarks for 1612. This piece, embossed with a scene depicting the Judgement of Solomon, is surrounded by a scroll border with masks between. The stem and foot, enriched with strapwork, masks and fruit, display a definite breakaway from the stiff Renaissance ornament, although some of its features are still present.

Later the decoration was no longer confined to borders but whole vessels were wrought in this manner. The style continued to develop under Christian van Vianen, the son of Adam, who was apprenticed in 1616 and became a master in 1628. Some of his works are unmarked, for example the piece illustrated, and others he signed A.V. like his father, which has led to a number of incorrect attributions in the past. In 1630 he came to England and in 1634 was commissioned by Charles I to produce a service for St George's Chapel, Windsor. Regrettably this was stolen, and presumably destroyed, three years after it was completed in 1642. An important piece

Front and back views of a ewer attributed to Christian van Vianen of Utrecht. About 1635

which he made on his first visit to England is a basin signed 'C.d. Vianen fecit 1635', now in the Victoria and Albert Museum. Its English origin is attributed to the fact that it does not bear Utrecht hallmarks, and as he was under the patronage of the king of this country he would not have been obliged to have it assayed.

This explanation can frequently account for the fact that a number of pieces of superb craftsmanship, of both English and continental origin, are found unmarked. The dish here is oval in outline resembling a pool, and bordered by dolphins with water gushing from their mouths. In the centre two more dolphins are seen gambolling in the waves.

Contemporary documents record that Christian worked in Utrecht from 1647 to 1652 and in London from 1661 to 1666, when it is assumed that he died, as no later records have been traced. The ewer illustrated is in the form of a snail's shell incorporating supple scrolls converging around a central cartouche depicting Perseus slaying the dragon. A bearded mask appears below the lip and Andromeda is chained to the

Dish attributed to
Christian van Vianen.
About 1630

Cup and cover, London 1666

body below the dolphin handle. The basin, on the other hand, is a somewhat more restrained piece. The lobate ornament appearing at the rim is centred at the apex by the figures of Bacchus, Ceres, and Venus playing with Cupid.

The style, which was adopted by other skilled Dutch craftsmen, spread to northern Europe and England, accelerated by the fact that in 1650 Christian van Vianen published a book of designs left by his father, *Les Modelles Artificiels*, engraved by Th. van Kessel. The cup and cover, made in London in 1666, maker's mark W.W., a fleur-de-lys below, is a combination of Dutch auricular motifs embellishing pineapple lobes of German inspiration. The piece illustrates how the style was emulated in this country. The silversmiths maintained the basic forms, using the lobate ornament merely as another form of decoration. Perhaps no English craftsman felt competent enough to compete with his Dutch counterpart in producing such elaborate pieces, or alternatively the full expression of the style may not have pleased the English patrons.

EARLY 17TH-CENTURY DESIGNS IN ENGLAND

In England in the early part of the 17th century styles did not vary enormously from those produced in the Elizabethan era, but two changes did occur. Firstly, decoration became more elaborate and covered whole surfaces, unlike Elizabethan vessels which are frequently found with plain panels alternating with ornament of one kind or another. Secondly, gilding replaced parcel-gilding.

The most notable alterations which took place were the changes in the shape of vessels. Gradually such items as cups and ewers became taller and tankards became larger. One form which evolved was the steeple cup, which takes its name from the steeple finial surmounting the cover. These finials are usually of triangular section, cast and pierced, or composed of sheets of silver soldered together, engraved or left plain.

An example is the Cunliffe Cup, by the anonymous maker T.C. of 1616–17, named

The Cunliffe Cup. A James I steeple cup and cover. Silver-gilt. London 1616–17

after its original owner. It also displays other alterations. The ornament embellishing the body, cover and foot is engraved and not embossed, and the flowers are no longer in tight clusters but appear in loose sprays. The stamped borders and matted backgrounds are features of the earlier style which remained.

The Mendip Cup, now in the City Art Gallery, Bristol, is of interest for two reasons. The decoration on the tazza-shaped bowl is composed of a network of punched lozenges resembling Venetian glass of the period, known as *vitro di trina*. Secondly, the inscription records: 'from MENDEP I was brought* out of a leden mine* in bristoll I was wrought* and now am silvar fine'. From this inscription we know that silver was mined in Somerset during the latter part of the 16th and early 17th centuries.

One of the earliest examples of these cups, dated 1572, is at Christ's College, Cambridge, and Sir Charles Jackson records another with London hallmarks for 1603; these contemporary examples help to date the Mendip Cup, which

The Mendip Cup, about 1610. City Art Gallery, Bristol

James II sweetmeat dish in the Portuguese style. London 1619

is unmarked. Taking into consideration the ornamentation on the foot, one can assume that it was made around 1610.

By the second decade of the 17th century plate became plainer in design and gilding was no longer popular. Possibly the Puritan influence was beginning to take effect. An exception is the sweetmeat dish, London, 1619, which represents a style believed to have reached England through trade with Portugal. In 1604, when James I of England made peace with Philip II of Spain, who had succeeded to the Portuguese throne in 1580, trade was once more resumed with the Iberian peninsula. In 1626 when Charles I had to raise money, no fewer than nineteen pieces of Portuguese plate were consigned to the melting pot. The dish of 1619 combines piercing with punched ornament. The strawberry dishes of 1631, by W. Maunday, again of Portuguese inspiration, show a later development of the style. A characteristic of this period was the light gauge of metal used. This particular form of decoration helped to strengthen the pieces.

Patterns most frequently encountered are clusters resembling fruit or flowers within panels, or spiral beading radiating from the centre. Whether the later dishes were used for strawberries is left to conjecture. We do know that strawberries were cultivated in the 16th century and were noted for their particular flavour, which unfortunately appears to have declined somewhat since the dessert strawberry that we know today was cultivated as a hybrid in 1806. The term strawberry dish was used again in the early 18th century to describe circular dishes with raised fluted borders.

The handles of Charles I dishes are cut out of sheet silver and tooled to resemble shells or leaves. Others are cast, usually of scroll design; the wire handles found on contemporary wine tasters are another variation. Some of these measure no more than $2\frac{1}{2}$ to 3in in diameter and are frequently seen with punched ornament. Sometimes vine motifs replaced the more usual designs. Although these items have a certain attraction, the standard of decoration is frequently crude and lacks the imagination and variety seen in the previous century.

The so-called bleeding bowl of 1635, maker's mark R.P.,

Charles I strawberry dishes by W. Maunday. London 1631

Charles I bleeding bowl, London 1635

illustrates the type of vessel devoid of ornament produced in the reign of Charles I and the Commonwealth period. It is said that these bowls were used when it was the practice of surgeons to bleed their patients as a cure for a variety of ills. A number of American examples are in existence, frequently found with the initials of a husband and wife, dating from the latter half of the 17th and the 18th centuries. Produced under English influence, those of American origin are believed to have been used as porringers, hence they can be described by both terms.

Only slight variations of design occurred from one century to another. The early examples have straight sides; later they acquired a convex outline and were bordered at the lip by a narrow band. The only alteration in the design of the flat handles is to be found in the piercing.

The term porringer or caudle cup is used in England to describe two-handled vessels with or without covers. Today to avoid confusion porringers are regarded as having straight sides, dating from the middle of the 17th century to 1720, and caudle cups are of baluster form, dating from 1650 to 1690. The name caudle is derived from the warm drink made of wine or ale, mixed with bread, sugar and spices, originally served in these vessels.

The caudle cup and cover of 1656 stands on a salver with a

capstan-shaped foot. This is the earliest type of salver known and was the forerunner of an item which has remained in its 18th-century form to the present day. In the 18th century the capstan foot was replaced by bracket, hoof, or claw and ball supports. The border of the salver is embossed with acanthus foliage, a motif not encountered since the early part of the century, alternating with ovals and at the rim fleshy scrolls, obviously influenced by the lobate style. Similar decoration encircles the body of the cup and cover with corded foot and matching ring finial. The contemporary armorials are enclosed in a cartouche of crossed plumes similar to that shown on page nine.

The decoration of these pieces shows considerable skill compared with plate produced in the reign of Charles I, and paved the way for the more exuberant Baroque style which came to England after the Restoration.

Commonwealth caudle cup and cover, and a salver on a foot.
Silver-gilt. London 1656

THE BAROQUE STYLE

In the middle of the 17th century in Holland, auricular ornament was gradually superseded by the Baroque style. This found particular favour at The Hague, where the former had never been popular. The motifs were inspired by the great interest in botany at the time, although the exact representation of plants was not strictly adhered to. For example sometimes two or more different flowers are found growing from a single stem. The most common motifs are large flowers, especially tulips, and scrolling foliage, inhabited by insects, birds, reptiles and cherubs. A master of particular skill in the field was Claes Baerdt of Bolsward. Embossing was the most popular form of decoration employed as it suited the complex and exuberant designs. This decoration was no longer treated as an integral part of the piece, and silversmiths reverted to more basic shapes; this ornament was used as an embellishment. (One exception was the tulip cup; a number of these

Pair of table candlesticks, probably by Jozef Haverstam. Dutch, The Hague 1665

Casket by Lucas Draef. Dutch, Amsterdam 1657

were produced by the Ferrn family of Nuremberg.) It is, however, not uncommon to find the two styles combined in one piece.

One such piece is a dish by Johannes Lutma made in 1651 and now in the Hallwyn Museum, Stockholm. (Lutma had been greatly influenced by Adam van Vianen in his early years and produced many splendid pieces in the lobate manner.) The broad rim of the dish is finely embossed with rural scenes representing the seasons, alternating with putti. However each cartouche is surrounded by lobate ornament.

By the time the Baroque style had fully evolved, flowers and foliage covered whole surfaces. The candlesticks illustrated, which form part of a toilet service in the Municipal Museum, The Hague, and which were made in that city, probably by Jozef Haverstam in 1665, are a good example of the style. They also represent a design of candlestick introduced during the third quarter of the 17th century, which became universally accepted both on the continent and in England and continued to be produced for some twenty years. The decoration on the candlesticks is more unusual than the larger leaves and floral ornament embellishing the casket by Lucas Draef, Amsterdam, 1657. The casket, which may also have been part of a toilet service originally, is by a master of particular skill in this field and represents a true picture of the Dutch interpretation of the style, which decorated many items of domestic and church plate for approximately forty years.

In England the restoration of Charles II in 1660 acted as a stimulus to the manufacture of large quantities of plate. After this date no grave internal strife caused the massive destruction or melting of silver, and hence a relatively large quantity has survived in comparison with earlier periods. But refashioning still accounts for the disappearance of some pieces. Many styles of decoration were employed. One of the most popular was the Baroque, but the work of the English silversmiths frequently lacked the fine detail produced by the Dutch craftsmen. According to Charles Oman in his book on Caroline silver, a book of designs by the Italian Polifilo Zarcarli was another source of inspiration for the English makers.

An impressive item dating from this period is the wall sconce. Although earlier examples have been recorded they are extremely rare. Wall sconces were made in various numbers and as many as eighteen, dating from the early part of the 18th century, are known to have constituted a single set.

They are fitted with one or two branches and the backplate acts as a reflector. The one illustrated, made in London in 1687 by the anonymous maker T.I., is one of a set of six still in existence. The backplate is centred by armorials of a slightly later date and is embossed with fruit swags and acanthus foliage. Partly draped putti are seated on either side and a winged cherub mask appears at the apex. The scroll branch terminated by a ram's mask supports the drip pan and sconce in the form of four palm leaves. Another simple design found was composed of an oblong backplate, the sconce resting in a pan at the base. A third adaptation involved the use of an arm rising from a boss, the hand holding a sconce; obviously no reflection was produced by this design. An example of the latter, which is rare, can be seen in the Victoria and Albert Museum, London.

One of a set of James II single-light wall sconces. London 1687

LATE 17TH-CENTURY ENGLISH DESIGNS

The two items illustrated here are designs produced for relatively short periods in the second half of the 17th century. The first is a two-handled porringer. The body of silver-gilt is overlaid with a sleeve pierced and embossed with foliage bearing lilies, tulips and other flowers, incorporating birds, and the matching cover is centred by a bud finial. Unlike the majority of these vessels in existence, this piece is fully marked, bearing the anonymous maker's mark T.M. over a crown and London hallmarks for 1669. Of the few examples of this type of work which have survived all the pieces are connected with drinking, porringers being the most numerous. It is accepted that porringers and caudle cups were no longer employed for their original purpose at this date but were used for drinking and were the forerunners of the cup and cover which came into vogue in the 18th century.

The source of the design probably came from south Germany

Charles II porringer and cover. Parcel-gilt. London 1669

Two-handled porringer by John Segar. Irish, Dublin 1685–87

or Switzerland, as a number of tankards and cups in existence display similar ornament, but the pierced and embossed sleeves on the continental examples have patterns of larger proportions. Similar work appeared again in the 18th century in Russia, where it was not unusual for the craftsmen to look back a hundred years for inspiration for their designs.

The other porringer, flat-chased in Chinoiserie style, illustrates one of the most attractive innovations of the English silversmiths, and no known continental counterpart exists. Nearly all pieces which survive date from between 1680 and 1688. The source of this Oriental decoration, which was obviously the silversmith's own fanciful interpretation of the East, was the trade which flourished between the two continents during this period. The whimsical birds, exotic foliage and weird figures were constant features of the style. This porringer is not of English origin but is modelled after a London example and made in Dublin in 1685–87. The maker, John Segar, also produced two other pieces in this style, a toilet mirror and a pair of table candlesticks, which are now in the National Museum of Ireland. These three items appear to be the only pieces of Irish origin in this style still in existence.

For the first time the piece under discussion bears provincial

Coconut cup with Charles II silver mounts by John Plummer.
York 1667

hallmarks (the Mendip Cup was unmarked). The rarity of this item lies in the fact that the silver mounts were made by John Plummer of York in 1667, a maker whose work shows strong Scandinavian and Dutch influence. Mounting coconut shells became popular in the Tudor period and continued through to the end of the 18th century, but unlike the example illustrated the trumpet-shaped base was the usual design and the decoration followed the prevailing taste of the period. The coconut shell was either incised or polished and produced an attractive contrast to the silver or silver-gilt mounts.

The nut of the Plummer cup is secured by four escalloped straps and the matching lip rim bears a slightly mystifying Latin inscription, which when freely translated reads: 'Once the contents have been imbued with something, it will serve as a test for John Talbot; I belong to Talbot to overcome my friends.' The cast scroll handles headed by monsters are of fine quality, a characteristic associated with his work and frequently lacking in many London pieces of this date. The pomegranate feet are typically Scandinavian and appear again in the Norwegian tankard by Morten Finchenhagen of Oslo, 1686.

Although the Norwegian tankard is somewhat later in date, the shape of the body, the feet and matching thumbpiece are all features which had been fashionable for some time. The insides of both tankards are fitted with a row of projections extending from the lip to the base which were used to indicate the amount of liquid consumed. This explains the term peg tankard. With the exception of inscriptions and pieces made in York, engraving was not a form of decoration which found favour in England at this date.

left Tankard by John Plummer. York 1657–58. Victoria and Albert Museum, London; *right* Tankard by Morten Finchenhagen. Norwegian, Oslo 1686

Not all plate made during the second half of the 17th century was decorated. The London tankard of 1684, maker's mark E.G., a mullet above and below, is a plain piece of good quality and pleasing proportions. The design, larger than earlier examples, is typical of the period, displaying a tapering cylindrical body, with moulding at the base, a corkscrew thumbpiece and raised stepped cover. It is not uncommon to find these lids domed at a later date when the style altered in the early part of the 18th century. It should be remembered that this alteration decreases their value considerably.

Few casters have survived before the third quarter of the 17th century. The one illustrated opposite (below), made in London in 1688, maker's mark I.I., of cylindrical outline, known as a lighthouse caster, is another simple piece, the piercing at the foot and cover and moulded bands around the body being the only form of decoration. Its early features are the large geometric piercing, which allowed coarse sugar and spices to pass through freely before the invention of milling machinery, and the bayonet lock, which was replaced soon

Charles II tankard, London 1684

afterwards by the slip-on cover. Casters which were made in sets of three are frequently found with one cover 'blind', thought to have been used for dry mustard. The second example, maker's mark W.B., mullet below, London, 1683, is a more unusual piece displaying vertical fluting and cut-card work applied below the finial.

A point worthy of note concerning casters of English origin dating from about 1700 is the ornate piercing encountered, accompanied by engraving, usually of attractive designs of flowers and foliage. The lighthouse casters were replaced during the reign of Queen Anne by examples of vase shape or baluster form, when the piercing became more formal and appeared within panels, designs which remained constant for many years.

Matting covering large areas is another form of decoration encountered during this period. It was a relatively inexpensive method of embellishment, which must have suited many patrons when they were trying to

above Charles II caster, London 1683; *below* James II caster, London 1688 replenish their treasures lost during the Civil War, and at a time when the economy of the country was still at a low ebb. In England its popularity declined with the introduction of the Britannia Standard in 1697, but it continued to be used on the continent, particularly in Germany, for many years. The bowl and cover, by Thomas Boulton of Dublin, 1696–97, displays the ornament alternating with plain panels most effectively. The matting and lobate handles illustrate the time lag in the design of pieces produced in Ireland compared with those of London origin, a factor which is noticeable throughout most of the 18th century. An exception to this is Irish silver made during the early years of the century when Irish silversmiths had direct contact with the Huguenot craftsmen who settled there.

The vertical parallel fluting which became popular in England during the late 17th century was another form of decoration inspired by Dutch craftsmen. However, the English goldsmiths soon found their own interpretation of the ornament. Bands of fluting alternating with gadrooning were frequently employed. These bands encircled the lower half of tankards, cups and porringers and were accompanied by punched motifs and corded girdles. The cartouches accompanying this decoration are often rather crude and out of period, composed of embossed scrolls, acanthus foliage and scalework. The snuffers stand by Benjamin Bradford, 1698, combines both forms of decoration.

This example is fitted with a contemporary extinguisher and a pair of snuffers, used to trim the wick of early candles which did not burn automatically. These stands, which were introduced around 1680 and continued for some fifty years, were often made by silversmiths who specialized in the production of candlesticks, but the more usual designs encountered are rectangular trays, fitted with a handle and raised on supports. In later years when some silversmiths specialized in making particular small items it is not unusual to find the matching snuffers by a different maker.

above William III two-handled, covered octagonal bowl by Thomas Boulton. Irish, Dublin 1696–97; *below* Snuffers' stand, snuffers and extinguisher, by Benjamin Bradford. London 1698

THE HUGUENOT INFLUENCE

The influence of Holland, which lasted for nearly a hundred years, was replaced by that of the Huguenot émigrés during the last quarter of the 17th century. The Revocation of the Edict of Nantes in 1685 resulted in many Protestant craftsmen leaving France and settling in various Protestant countries, where they could find refuge. A number went to Germany, Holland and Denmark, and some came to England. The majority who settled in this country arrived when the Protestant king, William III, and his wife Mary, replaced the Catholic James II in 1689.

The struggle which took place between the native silversmiths and the foreigners was a long and tedious battle, which in fact had begun some years previously. The English craftsmen objected to foreigners becoming freemen of the Goldsmiths' Company, and hence being able to carry out commissions for wealthy patrons interested in procuring the latest styles

Pair of table candlesticks by David Willaume. London 1700

above One of a pair of salt cellars by Pierre Harache. London 1694
below Charles II wine taster by Pierre Harache. London 1684

fashionable in the court of Louis XIV, the envy of many other European countries. Among other things, the Huguenots were accused of using large quantities of solder, thus giving a false impression of weight; and of inducing some less scrupulous English silversmiths to take their work to the Goldsmiths' Hall to be assayed. But the final result is reflected in the work of prominent English silversmiths, who quickly adopted the new style.

A striking change which took place was the heavier gauge of silver employed. During the Baroque period, when embossed ornament prevailed, a light gauge of metal was used in order to achieve the designs. Now many forms of ornament were applied. Among these one finds cut-card work, and its later development strapwork, which became highly decorative. The fine modelling of applied motifs such as shells, leaves and masks, escutcheons bearing armorials and decorative handles were also prominent features.

The first Huguenot silversmith to gain admittance to the Goldsmiths' Company was Pierre Harache. He was also one of

49

Cup and cover by David Willaume. London 1707

the finest craftsmen. Among some of his more important pieces is a wine cooler of 1697 in the Barber Surgeons' Company. The body is applied with pierced strapwork above a gadroon-bordered foot, and the handles are in the form of female caryatids rising from leaves.

The two pieces illustrated are of more modest proportions. The first is a wine taster of circular design with an escallop shell handle, made in 1684, two years after Harache was admitted to the Goldsmiths' Company. The salt cellar of 1694, one of a pair, displays bold elongated lobes alternating with flutes and illustrates a later 17th-century version of the trencher salt. This style was abandoned during the second quarter of the 18th century and was replaced by a container raised on supports.

The table candlesticks and cup and cover are by David Willaume, one of the most prolific and successful of the Huguenot silversmiths. Between 1688, when he registered his mark, and 1709, he had gained sufficient wealth to buy Tingrith Manor, in Bedfordshire. The candlesticks of 1700 are relatively simple in design, displaying leafage at the bases and sconces and gadroon ornament embellishing the octagonal shoulders. In comparison the two-handled cup and cover of 1707 shows typical strapwork chased with shells, lozenges and billets, alternating with elongated lobes. The decoration is repeated on the domed cover, an alteration which took place in the shape of these vessels. As the lids became higher so the bases were raised, and by the middle of the 18th century a trumpet-shaped foot was the standard design.

The small bell-shaped beaker of French provincial origin, made in Metz in about 1715, shows similar gadrooning and strapwork of a somewhat simpler nature, and is a modest piece in comparison with many other French vessels made in Paris or the more important provincial centres. A good parcel-gilt example made in Paris in 1706 with a slightly later cover can be seen in the Victoria and Albert Museum.

Beaker. French provincial, about 1715

The next two items, a ewer and basin, need some explanation as to their use in the 18th century. At this date these pieces were purely ornamental and were relegated to the sideboard as the use of forks at table became the accepted custom, and thus it was no longer necessary to wash one's hands during a meal. Sometimes these basins are called sideboard dishes.

The more usual form of ewer was helmet-shaped, but the one illustrated, by John Hugh Le Sage, made in 1725, belongs to a small group of display plate made by Huguenot silversmiths in the Louis XIV manner associated with the court of Versailles. Its design appears to derive from the engravings of vases by the Huguenot artist Jean Marot.

Another ewer very similar in design, but larger, formerly at Versailles, is depicted in Halle's painting of Louis XIV receiving the Doge of Genoa in audience in 1684. Unfortunately it was subsequently melted down. The egg-shaped body of the Le Sage ewer is spirally fluted

Ewer by John Hugh Le Sage. Silver-gilt. London 1725

Queen Anne sideboard dish by David Willaume. London 1711

and strengthened by four applied straps, each rising from a calyx to a volute terminal from which garlands of husks are suspended. Acanthus foliage decorates the neck, stem and base. The massive handle is in the form of a double-tailed triton leaning against a scroll.

The dish, by David Willaume, is simple in comparison. The waved gadroon and fluted rim is applied below a moulded scroll border with shells and strapwork arabesques. The contemporary engraved cartouche centred by armorials dating from the early 19th century is of the finest quality. Unfortunately the engraver is unknown. An occurrence which often took place was the removal of coats of arms when plate was passed from one owner to another. Today many basins or sideboard dishes are no longer accompanied by their companion ewers.

Anthony Nelme

The toilet service illustrated, by Anthony Nelme, 1691, basically English in taste, shows a slight evidence of the Huguenot influence in the applied pierced cut-card work around the bases of the covered bowls. A review of the work of this prolific silversmith, who received many royal commissions, illustrates both the French style and the plainer designs favoured by the English craftsmen, which have come to be known as the Queen Anne style. This is slightly misleading, as the designs continued into the reign of George I. Nelme was one of the silversmiths who signed a petition to King William III in 1697, stating that the English craftsmen were likely to become destitute if the influx of foreigners continued. Obviously this was not a personal petition, as his success is recorded by the large quantity of plate bearing his mark which has survived. The majority of English toilet services in existence date from the last quarter of the 17th century onwards, and are made up of many pieces, the most impressive being the toilet mirror. One of the finest of all is the Treby Service made by Paul de Lamerie.

The service by Nelme also contains two large rectangular boxes, called comb boxes, a pair of small candlesticks and an extinguisher, two covered bowls, two square scent flasks, two pairs of circular boxes in different sizes, a pair of baluster-shaped toilet pots, a pair of circular salvers, hair brushes, and a rectangular pin cushion. The only other items sometimes found at this date are a ewer and basin. Each piece is applied with a silver-gilt monogram within a foliate spray and is decorated with gadroon and fluted bands.

The toilet services which came into vogue later in the 18th century and continued into this century are made up of a number of pieces with glass bodies and silver mounts. Gradually such items as nail files, scissors, tongue scrapers and other toilet requisites became standard fitments. They are obviously of far less value than the earlier services. Unfortunately many of the latter have been split up, as a pair of candlesticks, salvers or covered bowls will attract more potential buyers at a modest price than a whole service costing, say, £13,500, the figure achieved when this one was sold at Sotheby's in 1967.

Part of a toilet service by Anthony Nelme. London 1691

ENGLISH SILVER IN THE 18TH CENTURY

As we said before, plainer designs were preferred by many English patrons. For them craftsmen relied entirely on shape to produce elegant pieces. The most common forms were octagonal, tapering cylindrical or baluster, with mouldings at the borders and rims. It was obviously difficult to conceive the exact proportions required. Any imbalance of design – a cover too high or a body too large in relation to the other component pieces – produced a most unsatisfactory result. But this style, which appealed to the simplicity associated with English taste, has remained much sought after to the present day.

The table candlestick illustrated is a good example of balanced proportions. The only interruptions in the elegant lines are the simple mouldings which appear at intervals. The base is engraved with contemporary armorials within a

One of a pair of table candlesticks by Pentecost Symonds. Exeter 1714

Queen Anne covered jug by Robert Cooper. London 1708

formal foliate, scalework and strapwork cartouche. Made by Pentecost Symonds of Exeter in 1714, it is comparable to many examples of London origin. No provincial naivety is in evidence.

The covered jug of 1708 illustrates the baluster form so frequently encountered. It is by Robert Cooper, an English silversmith, who was apprenticed to his father, William Cooper, but the decoration of this jug shows some Huguenot influence in the cut-card work which embellishes the handle sockets and spout.

The use of these jugs is somewhat obscure. They do not conform with the designs associated with coffee and chocolate pots, which have long spouts, but smaller versions are believed to have been used for hot milk, served with tea in the early 18th century. The presence of a wood handle does suggest a hot liquid, so perhaps they were used to serve a hot ale or beer. On the other hand, another pair of similar design, by the same maker, of 1700, are fitted with silver handles, which are properly finished, unlike those covered with wicker which were left rough. This suggests they were used to serve a cold liquid. Maybe jugs of this design were made to fulfil more than one purpose. Today we tend to give particular names to items to facilitate identification rather than guarantee past usage.

Silver for tea-drinking

The early 18th century is associated with the wider acceptance of the new beverages (tea, coffee and chocolate) which had been introduced a short time before and which resulted in the production of a wide range of vessels hitherto unknown. The earliest English teapot, maker's mark T.L., with London hallmarks for 1670, is in the Victoria and Albert Museum. This tapering cylindrical vessel with conical lid resembles a coffee pot and has only been identified because of the inscription it bears: 'this Silver tea pott was presented to ye Com^tte of ye East India Compane . . .' By the end of the 17th century the teapot has assumed a more familiar shape, either a baluster form or a bullet outline, adopted from Chinese porcelain designs.

An English painting by Richard Collins entitled *A tea party in the reign of George I*, also in the Victoria and Albert Museum, gives one a clear idea of the various items in use at the time. It depicts a baluster teapot resting on a lampstand, an octagonal milk jug, a circular sugar bowl and cover, a slop bowl of similar shape, and an oval spoon tray. The last two are decorated with vertical fluting. Another piece, a rectangular tea caddy, is fitted with a bun cover which was probably used for measuring the tea. From this description it is apparent that tea services at this date were assembled at random; therefore sets by the same maker and date are exceedingly rare.

The teaspoons and mote skimmer illustrated are somewhat unusual. The design of teaspoons followed the larger spoons of the period, and by the early 18th century the Hanoverian pattern (handles with up-turned terminals) was in vogue.

above Teapot, covered jug and sugar basin by Richard Watts. London 1712; *below* Four early 18th-century teaspoons and a mote skimmer. Silver-gilt. London about 1707

George I pitcher cream jug by Meshach Godwin. London 1723

They were accompanied by rat-tail bowls. The purpose of the mote skimmer has not been clearly established. Following the design of teaspoons but with pierced bowls, it is thought that they were used to skim floating tea leaves. Later examples have pointed terminals. It has been suggested that the terminal was used to clear the strainer of the teapot. This piece, together with the teaspoons and a pair of sugar nips (resembling scissors), rested in a spoon tray. Teaspoons were not placed on the saucer as the latter were sometimes used for drinking.

The pitcher-shaped jug was the earliest form of cream jug, but it could also have been used for cold milk. Like the salt cellars, these jugs were raised on supports later in the century. As good early examples are rare and expensive, they are sometimes found converted from the body of a contemporary caster with an added handle and spout. This is a relatively easy alteration and difficult for an inexperienced eye to detect. If one appears bearing a maker's mark associated with casters it should be viewed with suspicion and the construction of the spout carefully examined.

The other important vessels associated with the new beverages are coffee pots and chocolate pots. These are identical in every way with the exception of the finial of the chocolate pots, which can be removed to allow a rod to be inserted to stir up the chocolate. 18th-century chocolate, unlike that used today, did not dissolve automatically. The shapes followed the designs of other vessels and were either plain, or decorated in the prevailing fashion of the period. The spouts, sometimes faceted, were straight or curved in outline, often terminating in a moulding resembling a bird's head.

Sugar bowls similar to the one illustrated, with a ring finial or foot, had a dual purpose: the cover could be reversed and used as a spoon tray. Tea kettles which were also used at this time assumed the shape of teapots on lampstands, but were of larger proportions. A few resting on tripod tables are known to exist. In the second half of the 18th century they were replaced by tea urns, large vessels fitted with a heating iron, from which the contents were extracted through a spigot.

Silver for the dining table
As well as the vessels used for the new beverages the dinner table also acquired many additions during the early part of

Sugar bowl and cover by Edward Cornock. London 1728

One of a pair of double-lipped sauce boats by Anthony Nelme. London 1721

the 18th century, including soup tureens, sauce boats, cruet frames and ecuelles.

Soup tureens from this period, which are rare, resemble the wine cistern with the addition of a cover. No doubt when the designs became obsolete they were one of the first items to be melted down because of the large quantity of metal involved in their construction.

Sauce boats were first introduced during the reign of George I, and the double-lipped design with handles at right angles, similar to the one illustrated, was the earliest variety made. This type was soon replaced by oval vessels with single lips and handles, on bases or raised on supports.

Cruet frames were fitted with two silver-mounted glass bottles for oil and vinegar, resting in stands, and were later accompanied by sets of casters in either two-tiered or cinque-foil frames.

Salvers at this date did not always accompany other items such as cups and covers, but were used on their own. They were raised on a single foot or on three or more supports, and many variations in the shape of the border are found. Circular, square or rectangular designs are the most common. A particularly attractive variety are those with escalloped or angular rims. An example not so frequently found is the piece illustrated, decorated with cut-card work on the base around the foot and engraved with armorials.

Dinner plates dating from the 16th and 17th centuries are extremely rare, but a number of sets have survived from the early 18th century onwards. The borders are either plain or decorated with gadroon or reeded rims. Some thirty years later waved borders were introduced. It is not unusual to find among large collections dozens of these items reshaped at a later date and with added borders. In their altered form they may contravene the English hallmarking laws. Dinner plates were accompanied by second-course dishes, meat dishes in varying sizes, and a mazarine. This is an oval pierced plate, which fitted in a dish and was used as a strainer, usually for fish.

The ecuelle, an item based on a French design, is rare in England and those in existence date from the end of the 17th and early 18th centuries. (Their precise use in England is unknown.) Presumably ecuelles of English origin started life with covers like the French examples, which were also accompanied by stands. In France their popularity was

Top of a salver by Philip Rolles, and detail showing the foot. 1702

Ecuelle by David Willaume. London 1711

maintained throughout the 18th century, when it was the
custom to present them to mothers on the birth of their first
child; hence they are known as *bouillons d'accouchée*. The one
illustrated displays a shallow bowl and flat handles centred by
shells. This shape prevailed throughout their period of production, irrespective of provenance, but the decoration of the
handles and cover changed with the fashion of the time.

Tobacco boxes

Among the many boxes made during the early 18th century,
including some whose original function is uncertain, is the
tobacco box. Tobacco used as a form of snuff was grated and
inhaled as powder. Many of these oval boxes exist, with
detachable covers, engraved with armorials or monograms,
otherwise of plain design. As in the example illustrated, by
Edward Cornock of 1723, the armorials are surrounded by a
strapwork and scalework cartouche. A slight variation can be
seen in the other box, by William Fleming of 1709. Here the
engraving is bordered by a frame of repoussé ropework
decoration. As the popularity of tobacco decreased around

1730, the use of snuff already ground took its place, and the boxes were fitted with hinged covers. However one cannot afford to be too dogmatic as to the particular function of a box while both insufflations were in use.

A few gold boxes are in existence but they are rare and generally date from the 18th century. They are usually smaller and shallower than their counterparts in silver. Boxes of materials such as tortoiseshell, mounted in silver, are also known.

By the beginning of the second quarter of the 18th century the styles of the Huguenot silversmiths and those of native origin had gradually amalgamated and it became increasingly difficult to distinguish the work of one group of silversmiths from another without reference to the maker's mark. In the Rococo period which followed, many of the leading craftsmen were of Huguenot descent and maintained the prominent position which had been firmly established by their ancestors.

Three tobacco boxes:
top Edward Cornock, 1723;
middle William Fleming, 1709;
bottom William Fleming, 1704

THE ROCOCO STYLE

The formal, classical designs of the French Régence period (approximately 1700–25) were superseded by the Rococo style which again originated in France and involved the use of highly elaborate asymmetrical ornament based on natural forms and incorporating rock, shell, plant and marine motifs.

One of the greatest exponents of this extravagant decoration was Juste-Aurèle Meissonnier (1695–1750). Born in Turin, he moved to Paris and was admitted to the goldsmiths' guild in 1725. The only known piece which has survived bearing his mark is a gold snuff box with Paris hallmarks for 1728, but a number of his engravings for designs in silver are in existence; one example is the candlestick reproduced. A three-light candelabrum after this engraving, by Claude Duvivier, Paris, 1734–35, is in the Musée des Arts Décoratifs, Paris.

Other Parisian silversmiths of world fame are Thomas Germain and his son, François-Thomas, who produced some

Design for a table candlestick by Juste-Aurèle Meissonnier

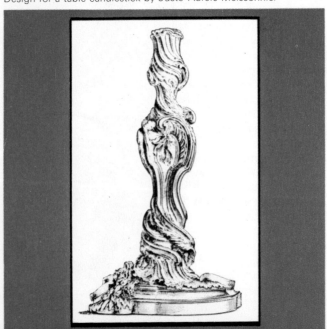

One of a pair of spice boxes from the Berkeley Castle dinner service, by Jacques Roettiers. Paris 1737

of the most remarkable creations in this style. As a large proportion of 18th-century French silver was destroyed during the Revolution of 1789, it was fortunate for posterity that both father and son worked for the kings of Portugal. A most extensive collection by these makers which has been preserved is in the Museo Nacional de Arte Antiga, Lisbon. A visit to this museum convinces one of the superb craftsmanship displayed by these makers. Thomas Germain held apartments in the Louvre as well as a separate shop in Paris and employed a large staff. He was obviously a prolific maker, but of the relatively small number of pieces of his work which have survived some bear his son's mark, making identification difficult. It appears that when François-Thomas inherited his father's position at the age of twenty-two he stamped his mark on a number of his father's works. François-Thomas, who benefited from his father's skill and reputation, came to a disastrous end through extravagance. He was declared bankrupt in 1765 and consequently lost his royal appointments. He died in obscurity in 1791.

Another notable Parisian silversmith, Jacques Roettiers, who was apprenticed to Germain, and another royal goldsmith, Nicolas Besnier, whose daughter he subsequently married, made the famous Berkeley Castle dinner service between 1735 and 1738. The trefoil-shaped spice box illustrated is one of a pair from this service. The revolving covers are encrusted with shells and flowers, and *rocaille* ornament encases the bodies. The service, consisting of approximately 141 pieces including soup tureens, table candlesticks, casters, cruet frames, 52 pieces of table silver, meat dishes, dinner plates and second-course dishes, was sold at Sotheby's in 1960 and fetched a world record price of £207,000.

Paul de Lamerie

The Rococo period in England is associated with the most sought-after English maker, Paul de Lamerie, whose best works were in this style. The son of a second generation Huguenot he was apprenticed to another Huguenot, Pierre Platel, in 1703, and was made a freeman of the Goldsmiths' Company in 1712, having served his seven years apprentice-

Sideboard dish by Paul de Lamerie. 1736

Salver by Paul de Lamerie. London 1737

ship. His success is recorded by the number of pieces still in existence in livery companies, museums and private collections. His early works were either in the Queen Anne style or the French Régence manner, but he later developed the asymmetrical designs associated with the Rococo style.

The four pieces illustrated have been taken from the later period, when his finest works were produced. The first, a sideboard dish of 1736, has a border applied and chased with emblems of the Four Elements interspersed with fish and shells, all linked with garlands of flowers and alternating with grotesque masks at the rim. The centre is applied with a contemporary coat of arms within a cartouche echoing the ornament on the rim. This piece represents the heavy cast and applied work at which de Lamerie excelled.

The salver of 1737 illustrates another mode of decoration, displaying engraving and flat chasing. A band of *rocaille* motifs and scrolls appears below the matching fluted rim, and the centre is engraved with a monogram within a typical asymmetrical cartouche.

Set of three casters in sizes by Paul de Lamerie. 1738

The controversy as to whether armorials and their accompanying cartouches were executed by the silversmiths or were farmed out to engravers will probably continue, but the engraving and other decoration on works by de Lamerie executed at the height of his career are so similar in design that it is quite probable they were carried out in his workshop.

The set of three casters of 1738 contains a variety of decoration, yet there is sufficient restraint to allow the ornament to be appreciated. On the body the applied masks with feather headdress alternate with foliate swags. The bases are pierced between scale and shell motifs; the covers display piercing and engraving of diaperwork above scroll panels enclosing cornucopiae.

These casters are overstruck with the maker's mark of Phillips Garden, who is reputed to have purchased patterns and dies belonging to de Lamerie after his death. We do know, from the research of Philip A. S. Phillips in his book *The Life and Work of Paul de Lamerie*, that two auctions did take place, one of his stock and the other of his tools, patterns and shop fittings, but the sale catalogues have not been discovered. In his will de Lamerie stated that his journeyman, Samuel Collins, was to be paid a certain sum on condition that Collins fnished plate already in hand, which was then to be sold. Why these pieces made in 1738 should be overstruck with Garden's mark is difficult to explain. Perhaps they were bought at the auction by Garden and, acting as a retailer, he felt entitled to use his own mark.

The last piece by de Lamerie, a coffee jug of 1747, is in comparison with the other pieces simple in design. If it were not for the well-modelled butterfly finial and delicate leafage at the spout and handle sockets, it could be by any other English silversmith of the period. Throughout his working life de Lamerie wrought pieces of plain design but obviously his skill in applied ornament and other forms of decoration brought to English silver a standard which has not been surpassed in this country.

Detail of coffee jug by Paul de Lamerie. 1747

Other English silversmiths

Many other silversmiths who worked in the Rococo style produced noteworthy pieces, but none appear to have been as prolific as de Lamerie. The invention of hard-paste porcelain on the continent provided new ideas for the silversmiths and many novel forms derived from this medium were introduced. Charles Kandler, considered by some to be on a par with de Lamerie, was a close relative of J. J. Kaendler, who created models for Meissen porcelain; a connection between the work of the two craftsmen can be appreciated.

This is also true of Nicholas Sprimont, but his career as a silversmith was a short one. Born in Liège, in 1716, he was apprenticed to his uncle in that city. Although the date of his arrival in England is uncertain we do know that he entered his mark in 1743, but approximately four years later he abandoned silversmithing to join the Chelsea porcelain factory. Among the few surviving pieces by Sprimont are a set of four sauce boats in the form of

Reading candelabrum by Samuel Siervent. 1762

shells decorated with panels of marine ornament radiating from volutes below snake handles, resting on matching stands, which he made in 1746. Perhaps one of his most imaginative and fanciful pieces in the Rococo manner is a kettle and stand of 1745, now in the Hermitage, Leningrad.

The reading candelabrum illustrated, 1762, by Samuel Siervent, is an item seldom seen in English silver, though many Italian examples are known. The position of the arms of this piece can be altered by releasing a screw to produce the desired illumination. Although late in date for Rococo ornament the design is in good taste and not carried to the extremes which eventually led to its abandonment and replacement by Neo-classicism during the second half of the 18th century.

The two silver-gilt beakers by Aymé Videau of 1743 are from a set of four beakers in two sizes. Each piece is engraved with scenes representing an English country gentleman wooing the local farmer's daughter within *rocaille* cartouches, linked with baskets of flowers. They display engraved ornament which is somewhat unusual for the period when embossing and chasing were particularly favoured. The cartouches have a slightly Oriental flavour. Chinoiserie ornament, revived once more during the Rococo era, was usually engraved, chased or embossed, unlike the original 17th-century decoration which was flat-chased.

Pair of silver-gilt beakers by Aymé Videau. 1743

The Rococo style in Ireland

Irish silversmiths had their own particular version of the Rococo designs, displaying animals and birds inhabiting the asymmetrical ornament. The punch bowl by John Williamson of Dublin, about 1760, is decorated on either side with scenes of pheasants beneath a tree, dolphins and fruit clusters interspersed with the more usual motifs.

Other items associated with Ireland are spool-shaped dish rings, used to support hot dishes, which were introduced around 1740. The earlier examples were pierced and flat-chased. Within a short time the chasing was replaced by embossing, frequently displaying farmyard scenes. Similar subjects are also found decorating oval spoon trays and circular sugar bowls which have survived in relatively large numbers.

Another piece often encountered is the helmet-shaped cream jug dating from the middle of the century, usually raised on three paw feet, headed by lion masks.

Scotland

As in Ireland certain pieces of Scottish origin dating from this period are easily recognised and one particular item is the

Punch bowl by John Williamson. Irish, Dublin about 1760

Teapot by Edward Lothian. Scottish, Edinburgh 1743

bullet-shaped teapot. The example reproduced is by Edward Lothian of Edinburgh of 1743. These teapots were first introduced in the early part of the 18th century and continued to be made for some sixty years. The shape of the body remained consistent throughout. Those of an early date were fitted with straight spouts, which were later replaced by fluted examples of curved outline. The decoration, which was either engraved or flat-chased, bordered the upper rim of the body and lip of the cover. This ornament was repeated on the everted lips of the oval cream boats (resembling sauce boats, but of smaller proportions), and circular sugar bowls which accompanied the teapots.

Another item associated with Scotland dating from this period, frequently unmarked, or bearing only a maker's mark, is a snuff box of oval outline, approximately $2\frac{1}{2}$ to 3in high. The Rococo ornament appears below the flat hinged lid and above the base.

Scandinavia

The Rococo style did not appear in Sweden until the middle of the 18th century. The impetus was provided partly by the arrival of Louisa Ulrika of Prussia, sister of Frederick the Great, who became the wife of Adolphus Fredrick. With her arrival the furnishing of the Stockholm palace was once more a matter of importance, and contact was made with French artists and craftsmen. However, the Swedish silversmiths quickly developed their own distinctive traits.

In Sweden beakers continued to be produced in large numbers, and to a lesser degree tankards, but it was the vessels connected with tea and coffee which displayed the most attractive designs. Teapots continued to be made resembling kettles but of smaller size, either without a foot, or with moulding at the base. It was not until about 1770 that they were raised on supports echoing the foliage embossed on the bodies. Two distinct styles of coffee pot were made. The earlier type of oval outline rested on domed bases and later, when supports were introduced, the shape altered to a circular design. The decoration was confined to floral sprays, *rocaille* ornament and moulding as seen on the coffee pot illustrated, by Magnus Graffe, about 1765. This maker worked in Göteborg and later moved to St Petersburg. As the pot bears a maker's mark only, one cannot establish with certainty its country of origin, but there is no doubt that the design is of Swedish derivation.

The Danish coffee pot, by Neils Johnsen, Copenhagen, of 1741, which was originally accompanied by an oval stand, illustrates another type of design, displaying vertical fluted panels. This form of decoration later developed during the Rococo period into spiral ornament, frequently accompanied by *rocaille* motifs of a rather coarse nature. The two patterns did not blend, unlike pieces made in Sweden, where they are seen to complement each other. A more pleasing form of ornament found in Denmark at this time was inspired by the work of French craftsmen, displaying finely matted floral tendrils and C-scrolls of symmetrical outline, sparingly applied.

The Norwegian silversmiths closely followed their Danish neighbours, but the Rococo influence was not in evidence until some years later.

above Coffee pot by Magnus Graffe. About 1765; *below* Coffee pot by Niels Johnsen. Danish, Copenhagen 1741

Germany

A sentiment often expressed in England is that German silver is too ornate. One cannot deny that the decoration is frequently elaborate, but many pieces displaying fine craftsmanship were produced. There are a number of distinctive styles associated with various towns, but obviously it would be impossible to discuss the wide variety in detail. The two examples reproduced serve to illustrate the dissimilarity of ornament found in two different regions.

The first example is of north German origin, made in Esens in about 1770 by Henricus Remmers. The body is chased with floral sprays and fluting, which are repeated on the domed cover and at the short spout.

The second coffee pot represents one of the most consistent designs produced in Augsburg, where more silver was wrought in the 18th century than in any other German centre. Made by J. C. Neuss in about 1775, this piece displays curved fluting encircling the body,

above Coffee pot by Henricus Remmers. North German, Esens about 1770; *below* Coffee pot by J. C. Neuss. South German, Augsburg, about 1775 and the only break occurs at the spout which is embellished with moulding.

Many noteworthy pieces were made in Augsburg. An outstanding maker of the period was Gottlied Satzger who, together with J.G.Klosse, produced a toilet service in 1755–57 which is now in the Wurttembergisches Landesmuseum, Stuttgart.

Switzerland

With few exceptions the silver made in Switzerland during the Rococo period is devoid of chasing and repoussé work. The shape of many pieces of domestic plate, such as coffee pots, meat dishes and ecuelles followed French designs, one example being the coffee pot illustrated, made in Geneva in about 1750.

A characteristic not found on French pots is the double moulding of the cartouches applied above the feet. Also many examples of French origin display some form of decoration at the spout, whereas the ornament on those by Swiss makers is normally confined to a moulded band near the body.

Coffee pot. Swiss, Geneva, about 1750

Holland

Although a certain amount of Dutch silver is spirally fluted and chased in the Rococo style, a more distinctive characteristic, connected with silversmiths working in The Hague, is the application of leaves decorating borders, forming covers, handles and supports. The coffee pot reproduced has leaves forming the feet and cover and in this instance is combined with spiral fluting encircling the body. It closely resembles the next example made in the Cape.

South Africa

Although little silver was made in the Cape during the 18th century, the pieces which have survived show strong Dutch influence. But judging from the research of David Heller the majority of silversmiths were of German origin. This is true of the four most important families of silversmiths – Lotter, Schmidt, Combrink and Vos – who all produced generations of craftsmen. Perhaps the Dutch influence can be accounted for by the fact that they may have served their apprenticeships in Holland, or alternatively these early designs were copies of pieces brought from their native country by the Dutch settlers. The maker of the coffee pot, D. H. Schmidt, who was one of the most talented, emigrated to the Cape as a soldier in the Dutch East India Company in 1768 and worked as a silversmith between 1779 and 1811. His work can be identified by his initials, D.H.S., which are accompanied by another mark, a bunch of grapes.

Belgium

The coffee pot reproduced, made in Mons in 1774, is a typical Belgian shape. The spiral fluting is far more pronounced than that found in most other countries and sweeps from the cover to the base. Often the spout rises from an angle similar to the one illustrated so that it becomes an integral part of the design. Many Belgian pots are of large proportions, a feature shared with similar vessels of Irish and American origin.

Italy

The next coffee pot is a typical north Italian design, made in Venice about the middle of the 18th century. A characteristic

top Coffee pot. Dutch, Utrecht 1754; *middle* Coffee pot by Daniel Heinrich Schmidt. South African, about 1785; *bottom* Coffee pot. Belgian, Mons 1774

of vessels from this area is the pronounced ribbed and fluted ornament which decorates the body, lid and foot. Another point indicating north Italian origin is the hinge of the cover which forms a right angle with the upper terminal of the handle. Those made further south, in Rome, usually have long curved spouts, decorated with grotesque masks and other motifs at the base.

Malta

Italian silver played a major part in influencing the designs produced in Malta during the middle of the 18th century. Sometimes it is difficult to dissociate southern Italian pieces from those of Maltese origin. Due to lack of research in the past a number have been incorrectly ascribed. Towards the end of the century Maltese designs became more local, and among the prominent features are the hoof feet supporting the coffee pot illustrated, made around 1775, together with the flower-head sockets of the handle and twisted bud finial surmounting the domed lid.

above Coffee pot. Italian, Venice, about 1760; *below* Coffee pot. Maltese, about 1775

Covered bowls with similar feet and finials appear to be among the most numerous items which have survived from this region.

Portugal

Among the many Portuguese designs made during the middle of the 18th century one finds pieces of English inspiration, which is apparent in the two coffee pots reproduced. The first was made in Oporto, about 1775, and the English example is by John Swift, London, 1767. The architectural scrolls found among the more usual flowering foliage are one of the distinguishing features of Portuguese chasing.

The shape of the two pots gives one an idea of the close relationship between items made at this time in the two countries, and other pieces such as salvers with shell and scroll borders, casters and salt cellars on hoof supports, could easily be ascribed incorrectly if reference to the hallmarks was ignored.

above Coffee pot. Portuguese, Oporto, about 1775; *bottom* Coffee pot by John Swift. English, 1764

MID 18TH-CENTURY DOMESTIC PLATE IN ENGLAND

While some patrons followed the French fashions there were others who preferred plainer designs, as in the early part of the century, so the concurrent production of both styles continued.

The covered jug, by Edward Feline, 1750, with a wooden handle, used for some hot beverage, is an item not often encountered but is of interest because it illustrates the shape of mid 18th-century tankards and mugs. The baluster body on moulded foot, domed cover and openwork thumbpiece are all constant features of tankards which of course are without spouts. Double-scroll handles replaced those of S-scroll outline found on earlier pieces.

The capacity of tankards was generally limited to a quart or pint and that of mugs, which are similar vessels without

Covered jug by Edward Feline.
London 1750

One of a pair of sauce boats by
Samuel Courtauld. 1747

covers, to a pint or half-pint size. The baluster form, which
was a predominant feature, was the standard shape for coffee
pots, cream jugs, casters, brandy warmers (which are small
saucepans with wooden handles and short spouts) and many
other items. About 1780 the shape of tankards and mugs
altered to a tapering cylindrical design, which is somewhat
unattractive, and is reflected in the price difference between
the two styles.

The sauce boat by Samuel Courtauld of 1747 illustrates the
oval outline which has remained unchanged throughout the
years, but variations have been achieved by altering the design
of the handles, and the decoration of the rims and supports.
The most constant pattern of handles is the double scroll,
capped with a leaf. The example by Courtauld displays an
unusual design in the form of well-modelled writhing dolphins, and the high standard of craftsmanship is accentuated
by the Rococo shells at the supports; both these features form
a striking contrast with the plain bodies with simple waved
lips. Sauce boats at this period frequently display little
aesthetic interest, but this is not true of this pair which

illustrate a high standard of craftsmanship, both in design and execution.

Candlesticks dating from the second quarter of the 18th century onwards have survived in considerable numbers. No doubt pairs in existence today originated from larger sets which have been split up over the years. From the similarity in the design of these cast examples it is obvious that they were made from similar moulds, and a number were produced by the silversmiths Ebenezer Coker, John and William Cafe and James and William Gould.

The first candlestick, by James Gould of 1738, measuring 7in in height, closely resembles those of an earlier date with the exception of the ribbed and fluted ornament bordering the base which is repeated again at the shoulder. Gradually as time progressed they became more ornate and taller, which is apparent from the second example of 1745, by William Gould, the son of James. This candlestick is embellished with Rococo ornament at the

above One of a pair of table candlesticks by James Gould. 1738; *below* One of a pair of table candlesticks by William Gould. 1745

Salver by R. Rew or Rugg. 1762

shaped square base which supports a knopped fluted stem rising to a shell-decorated shoulder, and it is fitted with a matching nozzle. Detachable nozzles were first introduced about this time, and many early 18th-century candlesticks are seen with later nozzles, which are most unattractive. The addition results in an unbalanced appearance. A rare variety, known as a desk candlestick, with a base and sconce divided by a knop, but without a stem, are sometimes seen. Few have survived with the exception of Sheffield plate examples, dating from about 1820.

Tapersticks followed the various patterns of candlesticks but were of dwarf size. A design of particular interest has a stem in the form of a harlequin standing on an ornate base with up-stretched arms, supporting a sconce and nozzle.

As certain makers are associated with candlesticks, the same is true of salvers. William Peaston, John Tuite and the makers with the initials R.R. for Robert Rew or Richard Rugg are just a few which spring to mind. An amusing rhyme has been written by the late Mr H. D. Ellis about the latter and runs as follows:

> 'Said Robert Rew to Richard Rugg
> "R.R.'s my mark", but with a shrug
> Said Richard Rugg to Robert Rew
> "I'm R.R. just as much as you";
> So neither yielded; both held out,
> And left the question still in doubt.'

The salver of 1762 by R. Rew or Rugg, engraved with contemporary armorials, displays a raised moulded border with gadroon and shell rim, one of the more usual patterns which replaced the shell and scroll, Chippendale or Bath borders of an earlier date.

The next item illustrated is a cow creamer by John Schuppe, a maker who specialized in these jugs; the majority were produced between 1757 and 1770. The design remained consistent throughout and the only notable variation appears to be the areas tooled to resemble fur. Some of the bodies are decorated all over, whereas others are found with the fur-like matting on the spine and forehead.

The aperture used for filling the jug, in the back of the cow,

Cow creamer by John Schuppe 1765

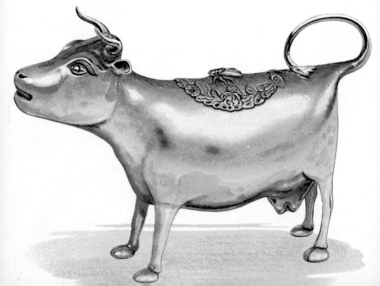

Dish cross by Coline Allan. About 1750

is fitted with a chased floral bordered cover and fly finial. Similar jugs were copied in Holland during the latter part of the 19th century and are worth about £40 in comparison with a good example by Schuppe which can fetch up to £1,000 at auction. Many variations were produced in porcelain too, and this is also true of another unusual item, namely the fox head stirrup cup, used by huntsmen, dating from about 1770 to 1835. As the name implies, they are in the form of foxes' heads, and some display most realistic masks, with tooled hide, bared teeth, pricked ears and alert eyes. A rare example recorded in the form of a hare's head was made by Rebecca Emes and Edward Barnard in 1809, and another resembling a hound's mask was probably made by Jonathan Millidge in Edinburgh in 1831.

As the dish ring was used in Ireland, so in England and Scotland dish crosses came into vogue. It is obvious from the example illustrated how the name evolved. Dish crosses had an added advantage in that they were usually fitted with a spirit lamp. Other features are the sliding supports, which enabled them to be used with dishes of varying sizes.

The following pieces are some of the more unusual items of table silver used by our forebears which always create a certain amount of curiosity and interest in collectors.

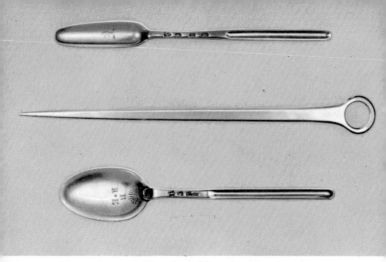

top Marrow scoop, 1725; *middle* Meat skewer, 1800; *bottom* Tablespoon with marrow scoop terminal, 1741

Punch ladles dating from the middle of the 18th century have survived in large numbers. The early examples were of circular form with a moulded rim, sometimes with a single lip. These were replaced around 1740 by a double-lipped design with ribbed and fluted bowls. Most had either turned wood or whalebone handles. The one illustrated, of 1752, is somewhat unusual; the bowl formed as a shell is chased with scrolls, flowers and *rocaille* ornament. Later a number were made out of coins and the base of the bowl inset with a half sovereign. Invariably this variety is unmarked and as a result is worth considerably less than earlier designs.

The three items illustrated above are a meat skewer, a tablespoon with marrow scoop terminal and a marrow scoop. The majority of meat skewers in existence date from about 1750 onwards and at first were of rectangular section. About 1790 those with sharp edges were introduced and are often used as paper knives today. The most common terminal is a simple ring which is sometimes decorated with a shell or replaced by a crest. A smaller variety was used for game.

The earliest recorded marrow scoops date from the end of the 17th century. These slender instruments, used to extract marrow from bones, a delicacy not so commonly eaten today, display two grooved sections, sometimes found with one indentation reversed, similar to the one reproduced of 1725. They are the successors to marrow spoons, which were ordinary tablespoons with marrow scoop terminals.

The example of 1741 is relatively late and illustrates another feature associated with spoons at this date; the back of the bowl is applied with an escallop shell. Spoons with rat-tail bowls had disappeared by this time and, although a number were made with a moulded drop below the stem, other motifs were beginning to appear; these were the forerunners of picture-back spoons which were produced between 1760 and 1780. The greatest variety of designs is found on teaspoons of this period, and scrolls, flowers, birds, animals and emblems are typical of the many patterns employed.

This ends a period in English silver when many of the finest pieces of plate were made and the influence of France which had remained pre-eminent since the end of the 17th century gradually died out.

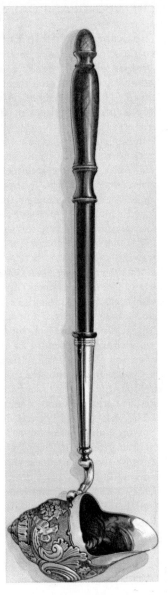

George II punch ladle by Philip Roker. 1752

THE NEO-CLASSICAL STYLE

The Adam period in England

By 1760 the time had come for a change. The Rococo designs were no longer fresh, and a style which had started as innumerable variations on a theme slowly became dull and hackneyed. The replacement, Neo-classicism, although elegant, seldom produced pieces of the same originality and artistic interest.

In England Neo-classicism is virtually synonymous with the work of the architects Robert Adam and his brother James, who extended their architectural style to furniture and the other decorative arts. It appears that Robert Adam was not commissioned by silversmiths to design silver, but he produced a number of drawings at the instigation of his wealthy patrons and these were carried out by craftsmen of the day.

The piece illustrated is one of the few items which is after a drawing signed by Robert Adam. The drawing was made in about 1763 and inscribed 'Vase for Thomas Dundas Esqr for a prize'. The name Thomas Dundas appears on the cup together with that of Sir Marmaduke Wyvill, Bart., both stewards of the Richmond races. The cup, known as the Richmond Race Cup, was made in 1764, by Daniel Smith and Robert Sharp, two leading silversmiths of the time. It was one of a series made for this important fixture in the turf calendar. The race was first contested in 1759. The trophy was commissioned for the last race run on the old course at High Moor in 1765; after this date it moved to Whitcliffe.

The vase-shaped body is decorated with a frieze at the lip showing horses galloping at full stretch and others being led by their grooms. It is applied below with two plaques representing equestrian scenes which did not appear on the original drawing but have been noted on a number of other contemporary race cups. Other features illustrate many of the ornamental motifs of the period, for example ribbon-tied festoons, stiff acanthus foliage, palm leaves and the Greek key pattern girdle on the spool-shaped cover.

The Richmond Race Cup. Cup and cover by Daniel Smith and Robert Sharp, after a deisgn by Robert Adam. Silver-gilt. London 1764

The pair of silver-gilt ewers and six goblets en suite, by Andrew Fogelberg and Stephen Gilbert are pieces of outstanding quality in the Neo-classical style.

Andrew Fogelberg, who was born in Sweden in about 1732, may have been some connection of the silversmith Petter Vogelberg (Fogelberg), who worked in Göteborg between 1720 and 1730. It is believed that he arrived in this country in about 1770 and went into partnership with Stephen Gilbert in 1780, a liaison which lasted until 1793. Gilbert, who was apprenticed to Edward Wakelin, was made a freeman in 1764 and worked in Panton Street from 1766 to 1771. Nothing is known of his whereabouts from 1771 to 1780 but it is presumed that he worked with Fogelberg at 30, Church Street, Soho.

The proximity of this address to that of James Tassie leads one to a possible source of the designs of the medallions embellishing the ewers and goblets, also noted on many other works by Fogelberg. Tassie, born in Glasgow, devised a method of producing both cameos and intaglios from easily fused glass by which means moulds from the originals and pressings from the moulds might be manufactured.

It is possible that the two craftsmen were friends and that Tassie either supplied Fogelberg with casts or allowed him to use the original sources for these designs. However, it must be remembered that most of the medallions on the ewers and goblets were also reproduced in paste by Wedgwood and Thomas Bentley, who were supplied with casts by John Flaxman and William Hackwood among others, as well as Tassie, and therefore their exact identity cannot be established. The ovoid bodies of the ewers and the bell-shaped goblets are embellished with typical Classical ornament – stiff acanthus foliage, ribbon-bound reeded girdles, beading at the rims and husk motifs on the handles. The weight of the set, which is approximately 207oz, gives one an idea of the heavy gauge and quality of these items, a feature not associated with many pieces dating from the period.

Bright-cut engraving (see p. 14) is found decorating an

Part of a set of two ewers and six goblets, with a close-up of one of the medallions. By Andrew Fogelberg and Stephen Gilbert. Silver-gilt. 1780

unusual pair of tea caddies of 1771, probably made by Thomas Jackson. Tea caddies were one of the few items produced which did not follow the more usual vase, urn or boat shapes associated with many pieces of Neo-classical domestic plate. (The word caddy is derived from the Malayan word *kati*, describing a weight of about 1½lb.) In the 18th century, due to various taxes, tea was an expensive luxury and for this reason the caddies were stored in a locked case. The two caddies for green and black tea were sometimes accompanied by a covered sugar bowl and less frequently one finds a set of teaspoons, a mote skimmer and a pair of sugar nips. The cases, often highly decorative, were made in many materials including wood, shagreen – a type of untanned leather originally made from the flanks of the wild asses of Persia and Turkey – ivory and tortoiseshell. Here the case is tortoiseshell, applied with a crested shield incorporating a lockplate, husk swags pendent from *paterae* and a mask flanked by foliage.

Pair of tea caddies with contemporary tortoiseshell case. Probably by Thomas Jackson. 1771

Globe inkstand by John Robins. 1800

The caddies, of cylindrical form, are engraved with bright-cut interlacing bands of laurel leaves and ribbons on hatched backgrounds, repeated on the flush hinged lids, centred by spray finials. The attractive Oriental scenes illustrate another period in the history of English silver when Chinoiserie decoration was revived.

The next item reproduced is a globe inkstand of 1800, by John Robins, a maker associated with these pieces. The design remained consistent throughout their short period of production, but the base of this one is unusual in that it is engraved with a perpetual calendar. The spherical body, supported on an openwork frame decorated with floral festoons, is controlled by the acorn finial which locks the two hinged segments when the inkstand is not in use. Measuring 6in high, the inside is fitted with a silver-mounted inkpot and sander, an ivory tablet and two silver finials for pencils. These inkstands are much sought after by collectors.

The tea set of 1786, with accompanying tea caddy of 1785,

by John Wakelin and William Taylor, displays a somewhat unusual design of octagonal outline. It illustrates both the uniformity of shape, and the various pieces, associated with tea services at this date. When this lot was sold at Sotheby's in 1964, it was accompanied by its original bill dated 18th January and 7th February 1787. Various entries from the invoice show how the value of silver items was assessed in the 18th century. One will suffice to demonstrate the point:

To an octagon Teapot weighing 17oz 8dwt
    at 5/5 per oz   £4 14 3
to making and engraving ornament, handle
    and button   £4
duty   8/9
                             ———   £4 8 9

                          Total £9 3 0

Obviously the duty refers to a tax which was introduced in 1784 and had to be paid on all pieces liable to compulsory hallmarking.

Teaset by John Wakelin and William Taylor. London 1785—86

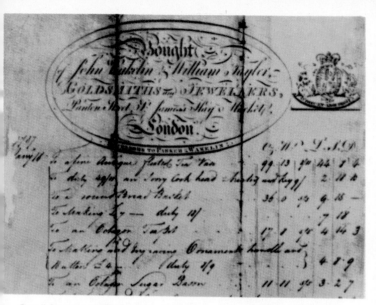

Detail from the original bill for the teaset on the opposite page

The milk jug, sugar basin, tea caddy and teapot on a stand are devoid of ornament with the exception of the crests and Greek key pattern bands at the borders. From other entries in the bill it is known that the service was accompanied by a tea vase (presumably what is known as a tea urn today) and a bread basket. Although the last mentioned may have followed the design of the set (as this was obviously a special order) it is unlikely, as baskets continued to be produced on their own as in former years. Coffee pots and hot water jugs followed the design of the milk jug; coffee urns resembled the tea urn, but were smaller. All frequently formed part of the service.

As the century drew to a close more and more tea and coffee sets were made, but it was the first quarter of the 19th century that saw the real rise in production that has continued to the present day. Obviously they were considered an essential part of the household plate. However the number that have survived, sometimes of rather poor quality, gives one the impression of mass-production, and therefore they are often less expensive than many other items of their period.

Hester Bateman

The work of Hester Bateman is avidly sought after by collectors. The cult has gained such momentum that any item by her is worth considerably more than pieces by other contemporary makers. Whether or not the high market value is a true reflection of her skill is a matter of opinion. She was the wife of a jeweller and chain maker, John Bateman, who on his death left the tools of his trade, the most treasured possession of a craftsman, to his wife; obviously he realized her potential.

As she lived with her husband, a craftsman, for more than seven years, she was exempt from serving an apprenticeship and she registered her mark in 1761. One must admire the speed at which she managed to establish her workshop and the domination she maintained throughout her life. Her sons John, who died in 1778, Peter, Jonathan and his wife Ann all worked under her and they did not register their marks until after she retired in 1790. The majority of pieces which have survived date from 1774 to 1790 as it appears that prior to this period she supplied other craftsmen. Her work is a typical example of the prevailing Neo-classical style, displaying the use of bright-cut engraving and pierced ornament fashionable at the time.

Her most attractive pieces are the small items such as nutmeg graters, wine labels and certain pieces of table silver, which show an individuality of style not apparent in many of her larger works. The salt spoons reproduced illustrate this point, displaying bright-cut engraving and pierced handles resembling entwined twigs rising from bowls in the form of well-modelled escallop shells. In comparison the tankard of 1783, in the form of a barrel decorated with reeded hoops, is a design which was introduced about 1775 and continued into the 19th century. However, the engraving of hopvines and barley ears shows initiative and adds a certain interest to an otherwise stereotyped design.

One of the finest pieces known by this maker is a silver-gilt cup and cover of 1790. From the date, one can assume that she could not have made the piece in her failing years, yet her sons

above Tankard by Hester Bateman. London 1783; *below* Salt spoons by Hester Bateman. London about 1780

and daughter-in-law, who no doubt were responsible for its construction, command only a fraction of the interest maintained by their mother. Her maker's mark H.B. in script must be the most widely recognized maker's mark in the history of English silver.

The Neo-classical style in America

Another silversmith who inspires similar interest is the American patriot, Paul Revere (1734–1818). He was the son of a Huguenot, Apollos Rivoire, to whom he was apprenticed. His career as a silversmith was seriously disrupted at various times by the political unrest in 18th-century America. During the lean years he turned to other pursuits, engraving and dentistry. After the War of Independence he resumed his original career and also started a foundry for casting bells. He achieved financial success during the latter part of his life as is obvious from the value of his estate, approximately $30,000, when he died in 1818.

In America silver styles generally followed English patterns.

Sauceboat by Paul Revere, and detail of the handle. American, Boston, about 1770

At first Revere worked in the plain mid 18th-century style, the style in which his best works were produced, exemplified by the sauce boat which he made in about 1770. His individuality can be seen in the delightful applied cherub mask decorating the leaf-capped handle. Similar masks have been noted on the handles of tankards with covers centred by finials. These are examples of the minor deviations found in American designs and are not associated with English work.

Later Revere adopted the Neo-classical style, illustrated by the caster which he made in about 1785, displaying an indentation in the lower half of the baluster body, beading at the foot, and a twisted finial centring the cover pierced within curved panels. This caster fetched $10,500 when it was sold in 1969 at the New York auctioneers Parke-Bernet, a high price when one considers the value (approximately £70–£80) of a similar English example by any maker, with the exception of Hester Bateman.

Caster by Paul Revere.
American, Boston, about 1785

France

The Neo-classical movement did not really begin until about 1770 but it continued well into the 19th century. The style spread quickly and a certain uniformity in design can be found throughout the various European countries during this period. France once more produced some fine craftsmen, among them Jacques Nicolas Roettiers, the son of Jacques Roettiers, (see p. 67), and Robert Joseph Auguste. As in England, the designs lack a certain spontaneity, but nevertheless the formal Classical motifs are well executed. The French work of the period is heavier than that of England, and bright-cut engraving, so popular here, did not find favour in France.

The tureen reproduced, one of a pair, is a fine example of the work of Robert Joseph Auguste. He became the leading French silversmith when J. N. Roettiers, whose house he bought on the Place du Carrousel, retired in 1777. Auguste's name is associated with many grand dinner services. The tureen resembles in design a pair of jardinières which form part of a service he made for Catherine the Great. The body is overlaid with festoons of oak leaves and acorns pendent from rams' masks. The borders are decorated with berried laurel leaves. On the stand and cover *paterae* alternate with matted strap-work panels. These various forms of ornament are all constant features of French Neo-classical plate.

Auguste was assisted by his son Henri, who inherited his father's appointments when the latter retired in 1785. Henri's best works are in the Empire style which can best be described as a development of the earlier designs, displaying even more formality and an extreme stylization of natural forms. The title associated with the Empire period is slightly misleading, as the designs were well under way before the Revolution. This is illustrated by a soup tureen, cover and stand of 1789–90 which formed part of a service presented to Napoleon by the city of Paris on the occasion of his coronation in 1804. It is now in the Musée de Malmaison.

One of the principal silversmiths who flourished during the Napoleonic era was Martin-Guillaume Biennais, but he can

Louis XVI soup tureen, cover and stand by Robert Joseph Auguste. French, Paris 1775–76

be more accurately described as a retailer as opposed to a craftsman. Due to the dissolution of the Parisian corporations or guilds during the Revolution, it was no longer necessary for candidates who were not sons of masters to serve an eight-year apprenticeship. Biennnais took advantage of this and within a short time was controlling an important silversmithing firm in Paris, employing some 600 workmen. His success was due to the patronage of Napoleon. Tradition records that he won the confidence of the man who became Emperor of France by supplying him with a *nécessaire* (a travelling box containing a varying number of items for the table and toilet purposes) before the campaigns in Egypt and Italy, and allowing him to pay after his return.

The supper set illustrated, by Biennais, is an unusual item. Those in existence date from the end of the 18th and early part of the 19th centuries; the majority of English origin were made in Sheffield plate. The four kidney-shaped dishes have covers

Supper set by Martin-Guillaume Biennais. Silver-gilt, French, Paris about 1810

One of a pair of toilet vases by Jean-Baptiste Claude Odiot.
Silver-gilt. French. Paris about 1806

surmounted by greyhound finials, and surround a shallow
central dish. Two shell-shaped salt cellars appear at the base
of the columns which are headed by winged female busts
supporting an upper tier, fitted with another dish and cover.
All component parts are contained in a revolving mahogany
stand. Like many other pieces from this era it is believed to
have been made for Napoleon, but there is no documentary
evidence to support this theory.

The toilet vase illustrates the work of Jean-Baptiste Claude
Odiot, who was descended from a long line of silversmiths.
He too received commissions from Napoleon. The bell-shaped
pot, decorated with stiff leafage and formal foliate borders, is
applied with oval shields bearing the imperial eagle above an
unidentified initial M. The formal decoration is repeated on the
finials and handles springing from bovine masks.

The French Empire style continued during the 19th century
and was still in favour when the throne reverted to the
Bourbons in 1814.

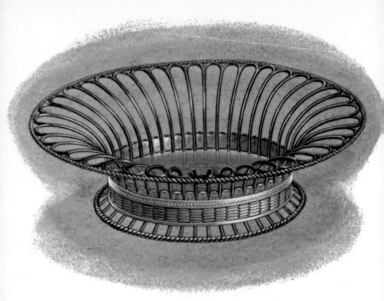

Oval cake basket by Paul Storr. London 1798

THE REGENCY PERIOD

The work of Paul Storr, another silversmith of outstanding ability, dominated the early part of the 19th century in England. Born in 1771, the son of Thomas Storr, a silver chaser and later a victualler, he was apprenticed to Andrew Fogelberg at 30, Church Street in about 1785. In 1792 he completed his apprenticeship and went into partnership with William Frisbee, an alliance which was dissolved the following year, when Storr took over the premises of his old master.

The first piece reproduced was made during the early part of his career, and illustrates the use of wirework which came into vogue about 1770. His early work, although attractive, frequently lacks the quality of this piece; here the canework effect is maintained throughout and accentuated by the band resembling basketweave above the foot.

Without doubt Storr's finest pieces date from the second stage in his career, when he was connected with the Royal Goldsmiths, Rundell, Bridge & Rundell. This organization received many important commissions. It enjoyed the patronage of the Prince Regent, later George IV, whose desire to possess massive and impressive pieces of silver can almost be described as insatiable. From the research of N. M. Penzer, Shirley Bury and others, it has been established that the Royal Goldsmiths employed a team of highly qualified artists. This has confirmed the view that, although the ability of Storr as a silversmith cannot be disputed, he must not be credited with the role of an inventor of designs.

Storr was appointed manager of Rundell's Soho shop in 1801 and by 1811 termed himself a partner. From the history of the firm by George Fox, a senior shopman, it is abundantly clear that Phillip Rundell was a most unpleasant master, whereas John Bridge was a diplomat and pacifist; they were appropriately named Oil (Bridge) and Vinegar (Rundell).

The silver-gilt butter dish, cover and stand of 1808 is reminiscent of the French Empire designs, displaying a girdle of anthemions within arches encircling the body, stamped guilloche bands and ribbon-bound reeded borders. Other familiar features are the stylized motifs flanking the paw feet

Butter dish, cover and stand by Paul Storr. Silver-gilt. London 1808

and the applied formal foliate disc surrounding the bud finial.

This piece however, although well executed, bears no comparison with the silver-gilt wine cooler, one of a set of four made in 1811, which is a masterpiece. From the research of Charles Oman, the history of the design has been established. It was the ambition of John Bridge, who controlled the design side of the firm, to provide the silversmiths with patterns by first-class artists. This he succeeded in doing by appointing William Theed, R.A., a sculptor, as head of the design department. Other sources were the work of John Flaxman whose pupil, Edward Hodges Baily, entered the organization in 1815.

The design for this vessel is almost certainly by Theed. The bell-shaped body depicts the Triumph of Bacchus. It shows the drunken Silenus carried by two satyrs, Dionysos reclining on a chariot drawn by horses and Persephone in another chariot drawn by a leopard. It is chased above the fluted foot with a frieze of acanthus foliage and bell-like flowers, interrupted by bearded masks supporting reeded handles. Vine tendrils are applied below the tongue and dart rim and on the interior of the lip.

Another wine cooler by Storr of 1808, in the collection of the Marquess of Ormonde, has a more ornate base and rests on a stand. A further set of eight, of 1808, was made for the Royal Collection by Benjamin Smith. Often minor alterations were made in the basic pattern to suit the taste or purse of a particular client.

Benjamin Smith was another leading silversmith who joined the firm of Rundell, Bridge & Rundell in 1802, and he managed their Greenwich factory until his departure in 1814. His early works were produced in conjunction first with Digby Scott and later with James Smith. In 1812 he registered his own mark. In 1814 he moved to Camberwell and was joined in 1816 by his son, also called Benjamin Smith, who inherited the firm after his father's death in 1823.

From a review of the work of both Smith and Storr, many pieces they made were of identical design, but examples by Smith are frequently slightly earlier in date than those by Storr.

Wine cooler by Paul Storr. Silver-gilt. London 1811

The inkstand reproduced, by Digby Scott and Benjamin Smith, was a royal christening present. The inscription records that it was a gift to Georgiana Stanhope, christened on 30th March 1802, from her godparents, the King, Queen and Princess Augusta. The daughter of the 5th Earl of Chesterfield, she married Frederick Richard West in 1820 and died at the age of twenty-one. The oblong base, raised on four well-modelled paw supports, is fitted with three pots chased with stiff leafage, which is repeated on the covers. In design it closely resembles another three-bottle inkstand, made by John Wakelin and William Taylor in 1790, engraved with the inscriptions: 'To the Lady Charlotte Finch on her Baptism' and 'The Gift of His Most Gracious Majesty George the Third'. A third example of 1808, by Benjamin Smith, with pots by Benjamin and James Smith, engraved with a cypher, also resembles those mentioned, but unfortunately its original owner has not been traced. Obviously the design was favoured

Inkstand by Digby Scott and Benjamin Smith. Silver-gilt. London 1803

by the royal household as a suitable gift for christenings.

Both Paul Storr and Benjamin Smith used their own maker's mark while they were employed by the firm in conjunction with the signature (often in Latin) of Rundell, Bridge & Rundell. After the departure of these craftsmen the work produced was marked first by Phillip Rundell from 1819 to 1822, and after that by John Bridge, who entered his mark in 1823 and died in 1834. However, these marks were a mere formality as neither Rundell nor Bridge was a silversmith, but each had served an apprenticeship with a jeweller by the name of Rogers in Bath. After 1834 the major commissions were farmed out to other silversmiths, the important work going to William Bateman, a direct descendant of Hester, and the Barnards, a firm which played an important part in the history of the craft during the Victorian era. After the death of Phillip Rundell, who left £1,500,000, and the loss of their great patron, George IV, the firm declined and was finally dissolved in 1842.

Domestic plate

The pieces which have been discussed represent silver made for wealthy patrons, but at the same time other silversmiths were carrying out orders for clients of more modest means. Some showed considerable skill, but their work often lacked the flair displayed by the Royal Goldsmiths. The items reproduced are not illustrated for the purpose of comparison, but demonstrate the progression of the Adam style during the early years of the 19th century.

The tea and coffee set by Robert and David Hennell of 1800 represents the work of a well-known family of silversmiths. The oval bodies of the service are decorated with bands of bright-cut engraving below the shoulder, replacing the floral festoons covering whole surfaces of earlier periods. Other alterations are the angular handles, and the flat base of the milk jug which was previously raised on a pedestal. The coffee pot has retained the vase shape of the earlier period, but as the century progressed it assumed a design resembling the teapot and the other accompanying pieces.

One of the most common shapes of the early 19th century was the rectangular design, frequently lobed and adopted for many items of domestic plate. Among the more recent additions one finds muffin dishes, bacon dishes, toast racks and a variety of goblets raised on pedestal bases. One also associates the period with the introduction of new designs in table silver,

Four-piece tea and coffee set by Robert and David Hennell. 1800

Cut-glass honey pot and cover with silver mounts by John Emes.
1807

namely King's and Queen's pattern, more ornate than those
previously wrought and the forerunners of a host of patterns
which came into being during the century.

The second piece reproduced is a honey pot of 1807, by
John Emes, an item popular among collectors. This example
is somewhat unusual in that the body and cover are of glass
with silver-gilt mounts. The borders are decorated with
formal foliage, and the stand is tooled with a Greek key pattern
fret, raised on anthemion embellished supports. A well-
modelled bee finial centres the cover. These pots, more often
made of silver, are frequently chased to resemble a beehive.

English silver during the Regency period was generally
superior in both design and execution to the work produced
elsewhere in Europe, with the exception of France, and represents, possibly for the last time, a standard of craftsmanship
which slowly declined with the introduction of machine-
production in later years.

THE VICTORIAN ERA

The reigns of King William IV and Queen Victoria, which together cover a period of seventy years, produced many variations in design whose origins can be traced back to a number of historical styles. To appreciate much of the work one must banish from one's mind the source of inspiration, otherwise comparison will lead to criticism. As new methods of workmanship were introduced with the invention of machinery, the fine detail, so much a feature of the past, was often lost. This is not to say that all plate was poorly executed, but that often the form is more pleasing than the details.

The pattern set by Rundell, Bridge & Rundell of employing a team of designers was taken up by other firms, and among these was the organization founded by Paul Storr. This firm and another, controlled by Robert Garrard, the Royal Goldsmith, were responsible for many of the outstanding commissions of the Victorian era.

Coffee jug on lampstand by
Paul Storr, 1829

above Spice box by Edmé Pierre Balzac. French, 1770–71; *below* Butter dish, cover and stand by Charles T. and George Fox. London 1841

The Rococo Revival

The second decade of the 19th century saw the revival of Rococo ornament. This is illustrated by the coffee jug on lampstand of 1829, by Storr. Although well executed and displaying typical Rococo motifs, the application of the ornament bears little resemblance to the original style. This piece is in good taste, but the jealous imitation of the style by other less gifted craftsmen resulted in some pieces of silver which are best ignored.

Another source of inspiration was the marine ornament favoured by such craftsmen as Nicholas Sprimont in the 18th century, as was the plate brought by French emigrants, who arrived in England, first after the Revolution and later after the fall of Napoleon. The two pieces reproduced illustrate this last point.

The Naturalistic style

The Rococo Revival led to the use of ornament based on natural forms. This developed from the application of handles and finials in these shapes – as in the coffee pot of 1829 by Paul Storr where the handle is in the form of a branch – to whole objects being wrought in this manner. Examples are the salt cellar of 1832 and salt spoon of 1835, by the unidentified maker W.B. – probably William Bateman. The body of the salt cellar is in the form of a convolvulus bloom resting on a base formed as a leafy spray. The spoon, with a similar bowl, is fitted with a handle resembling a branch. The style progressed and reached the height of its popularity during the 1840s. This is obvious from the number of centrepieces in the form of oak trees, dishes resembling leaves, and wine ewers, frequently made of glass, engulfed in silver mounts in the form of vines.

Salt cellar and spoon, probably by William Bateman. 1832–35

Octagonal bottle stand by Charles Reily and George Storer.
London 1841

The Gothic Revival

A few items of silver were produced in the Gothic style, which
enjoyed a massive revival during the 19th century. Its chief
protagonist was A. W. N. Pugin, who was discovered by
Rundell, Bridge & Rundell at an early age and later joined the
Birmingham firm of John Hardman. Converted to Roman
Catholicism in his twenties, he came to regard Gothic as the
only true Christian style. This is reflected in his designs for
church silver, signed by him and counter-signed by J. G.
Bridge, which are now in the Victoria and Albert Museum.

Although the silver produced in this style was mainly
reserved for ecclesiastical purposes, some pieces of domestic
plate illustrate similar designs. The bottle stand by Reily and
Storer of 1841 is one such piece. The octagonal body is formed
by Gothic arches enclosing typical tracery. The purism to be
seen in Pugin's work is not carried to such extremes in this
instance, as the border is applied with shamrocks, roses and
thistles.

The Renaissance and Classical styles

Two of the most popular styles which found favour during the middle of the 19th century were those based on Renaissance and Classical ornament.

The Renaissance Revival found greatest expression in the impressive shields and trophies designed and executed for the great industrial exhibitions of the day. Among the exponents of the style were a number of French designers, Antoine Vechte, Léonard Morel-Ladeuil and Albert Wilms, and the Englishman Henry Hugh Armstead. Vechte's early career was spent in Paris producing arms and armour in the Italian Renaissance manner. In 1844 he met John S. Hunt. He was later commissioned by Hunt to design the Titian Vase which was exhibited in Paris in 1847. Due to political trouble, despite his fame, he was unemployed when Hunt induced him to come to England and become a permanent employee of the firm of Hunt & Roskell in 1849.

Ruby glass fruit bowl with silver-gilt mounts by Charles Rawlings and William Summers. 1840

The bowl by Rawlings and Summers of 1840 represents a modest piece in 16th-century taste. The ruby glass body is supported by silver-gilt mounts displaying valance borders, chased with scrolling leafage and diaperwork and inset with semi-precious stones. The handles are in the form of goat masks and the piece is raised on an openwork base.

Obvious legacies of the Regency period were the ovolo borders, acanthus foliage and husks (which had never really disappeared from use) as were the friezes of figures of Classical inspiration. But whereas in the Regency period these had been embossed, now they were engraved or flatchased. Variations of texture were achieved by burnishing and matting certain areas, particularly the stylized leafage accompanying the scenes.

The wine ewer, made in 1860 by Messrs Barnard, illustrates a Classical frieze after Flaxman depicting Mercury and Pandora accompanied by stylized leafage. This is in complete contrast to the naturalistic treatment of the handle and finial.

Wine ewer by Messrs Barnard. 1860

Cream jug by Frederick Elkington. Silver-gilt. Birmingham 1875

The fortunes of the Elkington organization were made by the discovery of the method of plating silver by means of a galvanic current, patented by George Elkington in 1840. They were also concerned with the mania of the period in producing impressive pieces for exhibitions and rivalled the leading London firms.

They employed a number of French designers, among them Léonard Morel-Ladeuil. Born in Clermont-Ferrand, he studied under Vechte in Paris. In 1859 he was engaged by the Elkington firm and worked for them until his death in 1888. Among his important works is the Milton Shield, which depicts scenes from *Paradise Lost* in Renaissance style. It was shown at the Paris Exhibition of 1867. Its popularity, enhanced, no doubt, by the glowing reviews of contemporary critics, led to the production of many electrotype copies carried out by Elkington, an example of mass-production brought about by the technical achievements of the day.

The influence of Japan

A notable source of inspiration was the art of Japan which could be seen at many of the major exhibitions in the 1860s.

The craze was reflected in all forms of decorative art. In silver, the actual shapes of Japanese metalware were seldom emulated except for some straight-sided vessels similar to the cream jug by Frederick Elkington of Birmingham, made in 1875. The real influence is to be found in the decorative motifs the most common being branches bearing cherry blossoms (seen on the handle of the jug), fans, and strapwork enclosing geometric designs. Borders simulating bamboo, used three-dimensionally, carried on the naturalistic style and can be seen on the salver, also by Elkington, of 1879. This piece shows a typical Japanese-inspired design. The initials R.G., formed by branches centred by a bird in flight are a most attractive addition. Gilding and parcel-gilding are other features of the style.

Salver by Frederick Elkington. Birmingham 1879

left Table snuff box by Edward Smith. Birmingham 1853; *right* Table snuff box by Nathaniel Mills. Birmingham 1847

Snuff boxes and vinaigrettes

Among items of special note produced in the Victorian era are snuff boxes and vinaigrettes, associated in particular with Birmingham craftsmen. The first pieces reproduced are two table snuff boxes measuring 4½in and 5in respectively. They resemble pocket snuff boxes, which continued to be made, but these are of larger size. The sides and lid of the first example, by Edward Smith of 1853, display engine-turning, a means of decorating surfaces by turning metalwork on a lathe to produce decorative patterns.

Vinaigrettes were introduced during the second half of the 18th century, replacing pomanders of earlier periods. Their purpose was to ward off unpleasant smells. The interiors were fitted with sponges soaked in an aromatic substance and concealed by pierced grilles.

opposite Four vinaigrettes: *top* Joseph Willmore. Birmingham about 1830; *middle left* Gervase Wheeler. Birmingham 1838; *middle right* Rawlings and Summers, 1846; *bottom* Edward Smith. Birmingham 1850

Christopher Dresser

During the second half of the 19th century there was severe criticism of the current silver designs, inspired by foreign craftsmen and carried out by large commercial organizations. The designer Christopher Dresser (1834–1904) recognized the necessity for industrial production, but he aimed to promote functional and simple designs. In an article entitled 'Principles of Design', he pointed out that precious metals have an intrinsic value and therefore should be employed sparingly; this would mean that silver articles need not necessarily be expensive and would therefore reach a far wider public than before. Working freelance, his designs were used by Hukin & Heath, Elkington & Co., and James Dickson & Son. From the relatively few pieces in existence it is obvious that he was not accepted, either by the general public, who regarded the ostentatious styles as more to their taste, or the intellectuals, who disliked the idea of mass-production. But perhaps he was a man born ahead of his time; this stark simplicity was not seen again until the 1920s, in the work of the Bauhaus school.

The drawing for a teapot, for Elkington & Co., illustrates many of his principles of design. Using the minimum amount of metal, the body is formed by a cylinder, cut at intervals to produce the required shape. The decoration is limited to the rivets securing the overlapping incisions which are left unfinished. The straight tubular handle, inspired by Japanese work and joined to the body by strips of metal, is the only feature reminiscent of the past.

When mounting other materials in silver, he employed the same principles to produce elegant and functional items. This is illustrated by the claret jug of 1883, which was made by Hukin & Heath and bears their London makers' mark J.W.H./ J.T.H. The firm also worked in Birmingham where a different maker's mark was used. The jug is struck with the Patent Office Design Registry mark for 1881. These registry marks frequently appear on silver made between 1842 and 1883, and after this date were replaced by serial numbers.

above Claret jug by Hukin & Heath. Designed by Christopher Dresser. 1883; *below* Design for a teapot by Christopher Dresser. About 1899

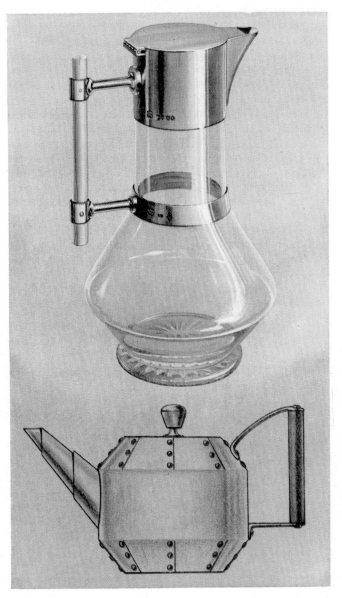

Art Nouveau

At the same time as Dresser was producing his designs for work on a commercial scale another school of thought emerged. This was an offshoot of the movement started by John Ruskin and William Morris which led to the foundation of the Arts and Crafts Exhibition Society. One of the most ardent followers, Charles Robert Ashbee (1863–1924) founded the Guild of Handicrafts Ltd in 1888. The organization was involved in the production of metalwork, woodwork, leatherwork and later books, avoiding the domination of the machine.

It was the designs for silver by Ashbee which were the oustanding achievements of the Guild, although, an architect by profession, he had little knowledge of the craft of silversmithing. As many of the Guild craftsmen were amateurs, or boys recruited from the East End of London and trained at the Ashbee school, much of their work was rather crude. His aversion to machine-produced articles is reflected by the fact that he encouraged his silversmiths to leave the hammer-

Two-handled bowl designed by C. R. Ashbee. Made by the Guild of Handicrafts. London 1902

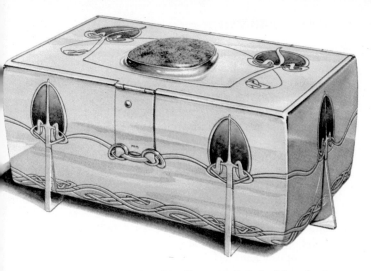

Jewel casket, probably designed by Alexander Knox for Liberty's of London. About 1900

marks on the surface of their work – a technique which was later adopted by other firms to simulate hand-wrought items.

Most of his designs are characterized by the application of long loop handles and semi-precious stones, the latter a feature of Pugin's work at an earlier date. Possibly Ashbee considered this the only idea worth salvaging from the previous era. These features are illustrated by the bowl which bears the maker's mark of the Guild of Handicrafts, registered by Ashbee in 1896. From contemporary records we know that he did not consider these designs as Art Nouveau, but today it is classified as such. The decoration of the bowl shows characteristic features of the style, but not the total involvement apparent elsewhere.

The casket represents the work produced for the firm of Liberty & Co., founded by Arthur Lasenby Liberty in 1875. Liberty used many metalwork designers, but as the firm's policy was to keep their names secret it has not been possible to establish with certainty the designer of the casket. However it has been attributed to Alexander Knox (1864–1933), one of their most gifted employees.

MODERN SILVER

As the Victorian era drew to a close the future of design was firmly back in the hands of individual craftsmen. One of the prominent figures in the early 20th century was Omar Ramsden. Born in 1873, he studied at the Sheffield School of Arts and Crafts where he met Alwyn Carr, with whom he formed a partnership which lasted for twenty years.

Carr's approach to design was the more progressive. His influence on Ramsden led to a gradual change in the work they produced, from pieces closely resembling those by Ashbee and his colleagues to an individual style easily recognized by its dependence on early Tudor designs. The hammer-finished surface favoured by Ashbee became more accentuated and is one of the principal features of their work. Another form of decoration seen on their earlier work was the elaborate use of applied gems and enamel plaques, often rather crudely executed.

Although Ramsden was a gifted designer, his drawings lacked finish and he therefore employed a draughtsman, William Maggs, previously a fabric designer, to carry out the drawings. As a silversmith student in Glasgow he was obviously held in high esteem, but his ability as a designer is paramount. Having completed four years in Sheffield, he joined the Royal College of Art in Kensington, winning many distinctions. His preference for designing is reflected in the development of his firm.

After a humble beginning in collaboration with Carr, who studied enamelling, Ramsden quickly rose to a position where he was able to employ skilled craftsmen to carry out his designs. There is little guarantee that any of the pieces bearing his mark, which he registered in conjunction with Carr in 1898, or his later mark registered in 1918, were actually made by him. Among his important commissions were pieces of plate for livery companies, ceremonial occasions and important private clients. Designs undertaken in other fields include the gates of the Old Bailey, ecclesiastical silver (including plate for Coventry cathedral), and church furnishings.

Rose bowl by Omar Ramsden, and detail showing the hallmarks, 1916

The piece reproduced, a rose bowl made in 1916, is signed 'Omar Ramsden me fecit'. It illustrates both the influence of the Art Nouveau movement and his preference for designs based on Tudor pieces. The pierced flower holder is made to resemble a Tudor rose with petals formed by the symmetrical mouldings in concentric circles. This motif, which he particularly favoured, is often seen in conjunction with castellated borders, angular knops inset with gems, and applied cable borders similar to that used on the foot of the bowl, all inspired by the work of 16th-century craftsmen.

Little is known of Ramsden's personal life. In 1927 he married a widow, Anne Emily Berriffe, under whose watchful eye the financial side of the firm prospered, but when he died in 1939 she was unable to continue. This was mainly due to the outbreak of the Second World War which resulted in the majority of the craftsmen being drafted into the army. So after forty years another organization which played a prominent part in the field of silver died, but the influence of this man is reflected in the work of many of his contemporaries.

Stuart Devlin

A leading silversmith of the 20th century, Stuart Devlin, has described his point of departure in the following words: 'Style and design had reached a point where no clear definition was apparent between the use of the precious metal, silver, and stainless steel, one being indistinguishable from the other without reference to the marks.'

His ambition has been to make silver the subject of his work, to make pieces which cannot be translated into other metals. He has a clear understanding of the qualities of silver, and of one in particular, namely its malleability. It is this which has led to the introduction of the new forms of decoration which characterize his work. Unlike designers such as Ashbee who hankered after the days of medieval craftsmanship, Devlin makes full use of modern technology.

During his early training in Australia, he was influenced by Scandinavian designers whose main preoccupation was with shape and form, and who avoided decoration of any kind.

Two candlesticks by Stuart Devlin. Silver-gilt

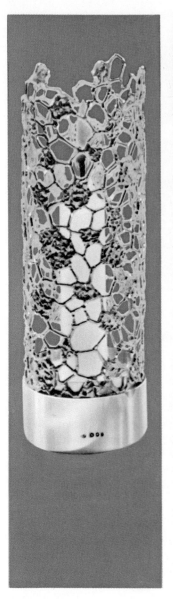
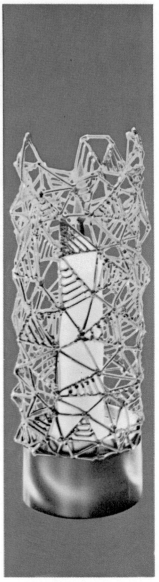

Ice bucket by Stuart Devlin. Parcel-gilt

Stuart Devlin has retained their clarity of outline while developing a delicate and intricate form of decoration, sometimes applied. At first this took the form of rather crude motifs based on marine life (fish scales, shells etc., technically known as crustacea) which then progressed to the fine abstract designs shown here.

In the candlesticks the ornament stands on its own. The first is fitted with a sleeve wrought from strips of wire forming a spider's web pattern. Another version of this design can be seen in the second candlestick; here the molten metal has been allowed to form rough discs of varying sizes which contrast with the fine wire mesh of the rest of the sleeve. Other variations are obtained by colouring the metal, either by oxidizing or gilding.

In the next piece we see a reversal of the process, in that the ornament is wrought from a sheet of metal which has been pierced and tooled, producing an overall symmetrical effect. In this instance the ornament is applied and combined with parcel-gilding, accentuating the contrast provided by the plain background and the finely punched openwork sleeve. From these examples the ability of Stuart Devlin as a silversmith must be clearly apparent. The control he maintains over his craftsmen in the production of every detail ensures a high standard of work, but one must also remember that he is the designer, the one who establishes the concept. With the participation of his team, his ideas become reality.

The last piece reproduced was designed for the Astor Award of 1972. This abstract object in the form of a sphere represents Life. It is pierced with three roundels which are applied with tooled oxydized spikes, symbolizing human force and ability, converging around a silver-gilt polygonal body, the soul.

These are just a few experiments in the field of silversmithing which have led to the establishment of new conceptions of ornament and which represent a complete break with tradition; they are the ideas of a man who looks to the future, and no doubt will be appreciated by generations to come.

The Astor Award by Stuart Devlin. Made in 1970, presented in 1972

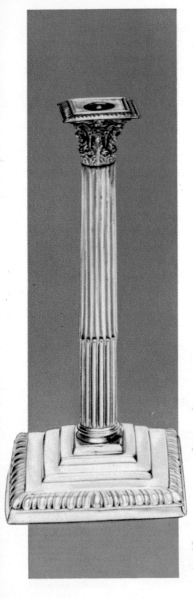

SHEFFIELD PLATE

The 'French' method of plating preceded plating by fusion. This was achieved by beating leaves of silver on to a metal at low temperature before oxidization took place. The next step was close plating, the only successful method of plating small articles with sharp edges, such as pieces of table silver. Before the article was applied with thin sheets of metal, cut to the required shape, it was dipped in a solution of salammoniac and then into melted tin. The surfaces were closed by applying pressure and finally a hot soldering iron was passed over the surface, causing the tin to melt, and thus to act as a solder. The process lost favour with the introduction of plating by fusion.

Tradition records that Thomas Boulsover discovered the process in 1743 while mending a knife handle. His attention was drawn to the behaviour of the metals silver and copper when heated. Here is a brief description of the technique. Sheets of silver cut to the required shape and thickness (which varied at

Taperstick. Sheffield plate.
About 1770

Double wine coaster with turned wood base. Sheffield plate.
About 1790

different periods) were placed on the copper and firmly pressed together to exclude air. Another copper plate, dressed with a solution of chalk to prevent adhesion to the silver, was placed on top. All three layers were bound with iron and put in a furnace, where fusion by heat took place.

The pieces which have been illustrated give one an idea of the variety of articles produced and also demonstrate various forms of decoration. Candlesticks, among the earliest and most numerous items of domestic plate, were a speciality of the firm of Winter, Parsons & Hall. The introduction of the Adam designs between 1760 and 1770 brought about a number of variations in style, mainly derived from the five architectural orders. The design of the taperstick reproduced displays a fluted columnar stem rising from a gadroon-bordered stepped square base topped by a Corinthian capital with detachable nozzle.

At this time both tapersticks and candlesticks made in silver and plate were loaded. This was done by inserting a rod up the centre of the stem and filling the hollow with a mixture of resin and loom. This mixture was replaced by plaster of Paris if the candlesticks were for export, as resin melts in a hot climate. Although this was a saving of labour and metal, the disadvantages are obvious. The thin shells with raised patterns stand little wear and as holes occur it is almost impossible for repairs to be carried out satisfactorily.

The double wine coasters resting on a boat-shaped stand, fitted with wheels, illustrate bright-cut engraving of about

1790. When this was first introduced a high proportion of silver deposit was used (24oz of silver to 8lb of copper) to facilitate the technique of engraving without exposing the copper. Later the proportion was reduced to 12oz of silver to 8lb of copper. The engraving was carried out by holding the tool at an angle, known as the side stroke, so avoiding the removal of an excessive amount of silver. A third step involved the application of heavily plated bands to the areas to be decorated, or soldering in shields, to facilitate the application of engraving of armorials and other inscriptions. This was achieved by cutting a patch in the metal, inserting a heavily plated shield, and concealing the borders by tooled decoration. Later the application of shields was replaced by rubbing in patches of fine silver. This was so cleverly executed that the only visible evidence is the difference of discoloration apparent when the piece becomes tarnished.

The shaving lamp, fitted with an adjustable slide, is one of the more unusual items

Pair of telescopic table candlesticks (one fully extended). Sheffield plate. About 1825

made in Sheffield plate. Not only were the craftsmen concerned with all pieces of domestic plate, but they obviously carried out special orders, which demonstrates the wide acceptance of the invention among contemporary patrons. Moreover, although originally a substitute for silver, Sheffield plate has considerable antique value today.

The last piece to be discussed is one of the many designs of telescopic candlestick associated with the craft. These can be raised or lowered by altering the height of the stem to produce the required reflection. The most common construction was that fitted with a cloth lining which facilitated easy movement and prevented scratching during the sliding process. The piece also illustrates the application of silver borders, which were made separately by stamping thin strips of metal with the desired pattern and filling them with a combination of lead and tin. The borders were finished in two ways, either by lapping over the silver or by applying a silver wire. This bevelled edge at the back of the mounts is one of the most distinguishable features of Sheffield plate.

Shaving mirror. Sheffield plate. About 1800

ELECTROPLATE

With the introduction of electroplate, patented in 1840 by the Elkington firm, the old method of plating by fusion gradually declined and within ten years was virtually extinct. Gilding by electrolysis was the first process to emerge employing the working properties of electricity. In 1814 the firm of Rundell, Bridge & Rundell used this method to gild a goblet by Paul Storr. This has survived in the Royal Collection, described in an inventory of 1832 as a 'Galvanic Goblet'.

Electrogilding and electroplating are the same process. The difference is achieved by using either gold or silver. A third process emerged on the same lines, known as electrotyping. This involved the attraction of a metal to a mould previously embossed and chased. When the mould was removed the decoration on the deposit resembled the original in every respect. This was the method used whereby many important pieces of display plate made for exhibitions were later reproduced commercially. The new invention was developed and controlled by the Elkington organization.

The use of copper was gradually replaced by nickel as the difference in colour was less obvious when the silver deposit showed signs of wear. The first step towards the use of nickel was the discovery of Samuel Roberts Sr who, in 1830, invented a means of applying a layer of nickel between the copper and the silver coating. A later development enabled the fusion of nickel alloy and silver. The process was used for the production of all types of domestic plate, and the styles followed those favoured by the silversmiths.

Many pieces involving a large quantity of metal were made in electroplate at a fractional cost to an equivalent item in silver, and so attracted a far wider market. Not only was the construction and metal a form of economy, but the decoration which was carried out by electro-damascening or etching (simulating chasing and engraving) required less time and skill than previous methods. The popularity of electroplate declined in this century with the introduction of chromium plate and later stainless steel.

Egg-boiler. Electroplate. About 1869

HALLMARKS

London hallmarks

A precise system of hallmarking silverware in London has been traced back to 1478. It is accepted that the date system was introduced at this time following the Act of 1477. It is also the time when the mark, a leopard's head crowned, was adopted. (An uncrowned leopard's head had been in use since 1300.)

The date letters ran in twenty-year cycles, using the letters A to U or V, omitting the letter J. It changed each year on 19th May, St Dunstan's Day, prior to the Reformation, and on 29th May thereafter.

Maker's marks were introduced in 1363. The early marks consisted of symbols, a practice which gradually declined in the 17th century when the makers employed their initials.

The lion passant, added in 1544, indicated that the silver was of the required standard. These four marks continued until 1697. Between 1697 and 1719 the amount of alloy allowed was reduced from 18dwt to 10dwt per Troy ounce. The marks used to indicate the higher standard were a lion's head erased at the shoulders and the figure of Britannia. During this period the makers were obliged to use the first two letters of their surname. The compulsory use of the higher standard was abolished in 1720; both standards have remained optional to the present day.

The sovereign's head was added in 1784, indicating that a duty imposed on silver had been paid, and continued to be used until 1890 when the duty was abolished. Although earlier in the 18th century other taxes had been introduced, no mark was used to indicate payment.

London *a* 1558 *b* 1697 *c* 1720 *d* 1786 *e* 1820 *f* 1838

In 1820 the leopard's head was no longer crowned. This mark, together with the lion passant, the variable date letter and the maker's mark are the standard London hallmarks today.

Provincial town marks

BIRMINGHAM The assay office of Birmingham was opened in 1773, and the mark adopted by the company was an anchor.

CHESTER When the Chester assay office was re-established at the end of the 17th century a regular system of hallmarking was introduced. The first mark illustrated was the town mark used between 1701 and 1778. The second mark continued to identify the town until the office was closed in 1962.

EXETER The town mark of the 16th and 17th centuries was the Roman letter X. In 1701, when a regular system commenced, the town mark altered to the arms of the city, which continued until 1883 when the office closed.

NEWCASTLE A regular system of hallmarking was started in 1702. The town mark adopted was the arms of the city, three castles. The office was closed in 1884.

SHEFFIELD The office was established in 1773. The town mark is a crown.

YORK This was the most important provincial city in medieval England. In 1566 the town mark adopted was a halved leopard's head and a halved fleur-de-lys conjoined, replaced in 1632 by a half rose crowned and a half fleur-de-lys. This was substituted in 1700 by a cross charged with five lions passant, the arms of the city. The office closed in 1856.

a Birmingham *b* Chester *c* Exeter *d* Newcastle *e* Sheffield *f* York

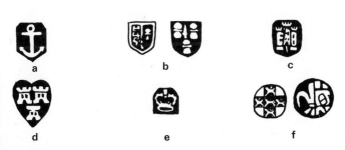

Scottish hallmarks

EDINBURGH From 1457 onwards the silver made in Edinburgh was required by statute to be marked with the maker's mark and the deacon's mark. In 1485 the town mark was introduced, taken from the arms of the burgh. The date letter system was adopted in 1681. In the same year the deacon's mark was replaced by the mark of the assay master, which in turn was substituted by another mark, a thistle, in 1759. As in London the duty mark of the reigning sovereign's head was introduced in 1784 and continued until 1890.

GLASGOW The most important Scottish provincial town adopted the burgh arms as the town mark. The earliest known marked plate dates from the end of the 17th century. In 1681 the date system was introduced, but it was not until 1819 that a regular assay office was established. The second set of marks illustrated represent the hallmarks used from this date until the office closed in 1964. The lion rampant replaced a letter, frequently an S, believed to have indicated the sterling standard.

Edinburgh *a* 1681 *b* 1759
Glasgow *c* 1694 *d* 1819

Irish hallmarks

DUBLIN In 1637 silversmiths were ordered to stamp their silver with a mark, a harp crowned, and their maker's mark. A third mark, the date letter, was added in 1638. A fourth, the figure of Hibernia, was adopted in 1730, denoting the payment of a duty of 6d. per ounce imposed on all gold and silver. With the introduction of the Hibernia mark the date letter was frequently omitted. Exceptions were spoons and forks, which were more often than not fully marked. In recent years, by comparing dated and undated pieces, variations in the harp and Hibernia marks have been noted, and a dating system has been established. The practice of omitting the date letter was abolished around 1775. The sovereign's head was not introduced until 1807 and was dropped in 1890, when the duty was abolished. The Britannia standard was never in force in Ireland, and no marks associated with this standard were ever used.

Dublin *a* 1658 *b* 1731 *c* 1807 *d* 1838

Continental hallmarks

Belgium

MONS   The first mark is the town mark used in the middle of the 18th century. It was accompanied by another mark in the form of a monogram, A.E., conjoined below a crown. These letters indicate the first letters of the names of the governor of the Spanish Netherlands, Archduke Albrecht, and his wife Elizabeth of Spain.

Denmark

COPENHAGEN   The town mark, three towers in an oval shield with the date below, was introduced in 1608. The assay master's mark was added in 1679, denoting the fitness of the metal. A month mark (not illustrated) was used between 1685 and 1825. The last mark indicates the maker's initials, and in Denmark was frequently accompanied by the date when the maker's mark was entered.

France

The hallmarking system in France was somewhat more complicated than that used in England, and more precise. From 1672 onwards a system of taxation was imposed on precious metal. This was collected by a tax *fermier*, who was

BELGIUM *a* Mons town mark, 18th century DENMARK *b* Copenhagen town mark *c* assay master Peter Nicolai V. Haven *d* maker Peder Hansen Klein FRANCE *e* Paris charge mark 1732–38 *f* date letter 1734 *g* maker Jacques Roettiers *h* Metz town mark, early 18th century *i* unidentified maker *j* maker Jean-Baptiste Claude Odiot

permitted to extract fees for his work. During construction the maker placed his own mark on the piece, and the tax *fermier* added the charge mark after the object had been registered in his records. Thirdly, the piece received the city mark and date letter, indicating the item was up to standard. After completion the piece was weighed and the tax paid. At this point the discharge mark was struck, releasing the item for sale. The application of marks at various times of construction explains why many French marks appear distorted. After the Revolution the old system was abolished and replaced by a new one, indicated initially by the Gallic cock and numerous other import and export marks. Pre-Revolution Parisian makers' marks were accompanied by a fleur-de-lys crowned. In the provincial towns various other devices were used. After the Revolution all makers' marks were enclosed within a lozenge.

Germany

AUGSBURG   Augsburg adopted the coat of arms of the city, a pineapple, as the town mark. In 1735 a system of date letters was introduced; each letter was maintained for two years. From 1779 onwards the letters were in force for one year only, and this practice continued until 1839 when this method of marking was finally abolished.

ESENS   The second set of German marks reproduced are the town mark of Esens, used in the middle of the 18th century, accompanied by a maker's mark.

GERMANY *a* Augsburg town mark, late 16th century *b* unidentified maker *c* Augsburg town mark 1775–77 *d* maker Johann Christian Neuss *e* Esens town mark, mid 18th century *f* maker Henricus Remmers

a   b   c   d   e   f

Italy

VENICE The town mark, the head of the lion of St Mark, was accompanied by the maker's mark and the assay master's mark after 1598. As the town mark of Padua is almost identical it is frequently impossible to distinguish between the two cities.

Malta

The Maltese marks reproduced are taken from the Rohan Code, named after the grandmaster Emanuel de Rohan (1775–97). During the period when this code was in use (1778–1856), three standards of silver were allowed: Maltese, Roman and French. The first letter of each word was used to denote the standard. Maltese silver was made up of $10\frac{1}{2}$ parts of silver and $1\frac{1}{2}$ parts of alloy. Roman silver consisted of eleven parts of silver and one part of alloy. The highest standard, French silver, allowed half a part of alloy to be combined with $11\frac{1}{2}$ parts of silver. These marks were accompanied by the official assay master's mark and the maker's mark.

ITALY *a* Venice town mark, mid 18th century MALTA *b and d* town mark, about 1800 *c* assay master's mark *e* unidentified maker

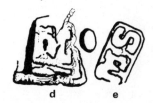

The Netherlands

AMSTERDAM From the first decade of the 16th century, Dutch silversmiths were required to have their wares marked with the city arms, a date letter and a maker's mark. In Amsterdam a continuous date system has been in existence since 1503. The mark of the province, a lion rampant for Holland, was introduced in 1664. In 1798 the guilds were abolished. After a transitional period a new system was set up on a national basis in 1813, and has continued to the present day.

DORDRECHT This town did not adopt the arms of the city as its mark of origin but a crowned rose. As in Amsterdam the lion was added after 1663.

UTRECHT The shield of the town was used. From 1712 onwards the town mark was struck twice.

Norway

OSLO The town mark of Oslo (formerly Christiana), a crowned C frequently with a date inside, is known from existing pieces dating from the early 17th century.

THE NETHERLANDS *a* Amsterdam town mark *b* date letter 1657 *c* maker Lucas Draef *d* Dordrecht town mark *e* date letter 1608 *f* Utrecht town mark after 1712 NORWAY *g* Oslo town mark 1671 *h* maker Morten Finchenhagen

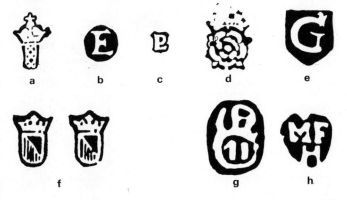

a   b   c   d   e

f   g   h

Portugal

OPORTO   Portuguese silver bears only two marks, a town mark and a maker's mark. The letter P illustrated was the town mark of Oporto. No date system was used, but the innumerable variations in the shield of the town mark help to establish periods with reasonable certainty.

Russia

The systematic marking of silver in Russia was not introduced until 1700. A separate date system was not used, but the date was incorporated with the town mark or the assay master's mark.

South Africa

Many devices have been noted accompanying Cape makers' marks but their significance has not been established. It has been suggested that, when shops were without fronts and few people could read, tradespeople hung identifying signs outside their workshops. Therefore the bunch of grapes illustrated may have been that used by Daniel Heinrich Schmidt.

PORTUGAL *a* Oporto town mark 1768–91 RUSSIA *b* Vologda town mark *c* assay master *d* maker SOUTH AFRICA *e* maker Daniel Heinrich Schmidt

a

b

c

d

e

Sweden

STOCKHOLM The first city mark of Stockholm was a crown, which was altered to the head of St Erik in 1689 when a date system was introduced. In 1759 the date system was adopted for the whole kingdom of Sweden, including Finland. In 1752 a state punch was added, represented by three crowns.

Switzerland

GENEVA Like much German silver, Swiss silver is stamped with a town mark and a maker's mark. The mid 18th-century town mark of Geneva illustrated is a halved bird and key above the assay master's initials. Swiss silver seldom bears an assay scrape, unlike that of German origin. This zigzag line was merely a scar left after silver had been removed for the purpose of testing, and has no other significance.

SWEDEN *a* Stockholm town mark *b* maker Rudolf Wittkopf *c* date letter 1699 SWITZERLAND *d* Geneva town mark, 18th century

FAKES AND ALTERATIONS

When trying to decide whether or not a piece of silver is authentic, it is easier to approach the subject from a positive angle. First, without reference to the marks, establish a date. Then, if on further examination one finds the article is completely out of period, one's suspicions should be aroused.

It is all too easy to condemn objects as 'wrong', and therefore careful consideration is necessary. After all, it must be remembered that until recently silver was made by hand, and if a craftsman decided to deviate from the norm in some minor way, this does not necessarily mean that the item is a fake. Many genuine copies do exist, made when a particular fashion was revived, or a special order demanded the replacement of something lost or destroyed. To discuss the subject in detail would be impossible, and therefore the items which have been chosen are a cross-section of the more usual alterations and fakes.

Mug by J. Kentember, 1768, with added lip

Two-handled porringer with let-in base, with London hallmarks for 1724

The first piece is a common alteration, namely the conversion of a mug into a jug. The mug by J. Kentember started life as a plain piece of baluster form. The decoration was carried out when it was re-shaped and applied with a spout. It bears an inscription dated 1882, which is probably the date when the alteration took place. In this state it infringes the hallmarking laws of Britain and cannot be sold.

The second piece illustrates transposed hallmarks. This is one of the commonest examples of forgery carried out in England. At one time it was done to avoid paying duty, which was 6d an ounce, enforced between 1719 and 1758. The offending objects are known as 'duty dodgers'. It was a simple process to cut the marks out of a small or damaged piece and insert them into another one, possibly much larger, so avoiding considerable expense. They can be detected by the style being slightly out of period and the presence of a solder line around the marks. Sometimes the insertion was carried out between the base of the body and the foot which is concealed by a genuine join. For this reason it is advisable to examine the inside of pieces marked on the base, as an impres-

Coffee pot by Seth Lofthouse, London 1718, later chased and embossed

sion of the hallmarks can sometimes be seen, confirming that a false disc bearing marks has not been inserted.

The porringer of 1724 is not a duty dodger, but a fake of a much later date. No effort has been made to reproduce the article in the correct style of the period. On examination a solder line can be seen around the base. As the bodies of these porringers were made in one piece, there is absolutely no doubt that it is not genuine.

The coffee pot of 1718 is not a fake as no additions have been applied and the marks are authentic, but the chased decoration represents the work of our Victorian ancestors who, obviously, considered plain silver dull and unfashionable.

Later decoration can reduce the price of a piece enormously. This has led to the removal of later ornament, a fact which can be quite easily overlooked by an unsuspecting buyer. It can sometimes be detected by traces of the pattern which become visible as tarnishing occurs. Another indication can be the slightly bulbous outline of the body of a cylindrical vessel.

This is caused by the de-chasing process which stretches the metal; also an overpolished flat surface is common.

The wine cup of 1780, which again started life plain, with the exception of the beading on the foot, illustrates both later decoration and additions. The strapwork is inspired by the Huguenot designs, and the chasing is in the naturalistic style of the Victorian era. This is an example where the original purpose has not been changed by the additions. Therefore, if they are up to standard, they can receive addition marks. This type of alteration is more usual on salvers which have acquired new borders and feet to suit current fashions. Sometimes the additions were marked at the time of alteration.

To conclude, the main points to watch for are the construction, the position and quality of the marks, and the colour and patina of the surface. Also the style of the piece is important. Badly proportioned component parts, giving an unbalanced appearance, are not features of authentic pieces, but it is only by handling many genuine articles that a specialized knowledge of the craft can be acquired.

Wine cup, later gilt and decorated, bearing London hallmarks for 1780

BOOKS TO READ

Bradbury, Frederick, *The History of Old Sheffield Plate*, London 1912

Brunner, Herbert, *Old Table Silver*, translated by Seligman, Janet, London 1967

Bury, Shirley, *Victorian Electroplate*, London 1971

Clayton, Michael, *The Collector's Dictionary of the Silver and Gold of Great Britain and North America*, London 1971

Culme, John and Strang, John G., *Antique Silver and Silver Collecting*, London 1973

Gans, M. H., and Duyvené de Wit-Klinkhamer, T. M., *Dutch Silver*, translated by van Oss, Oliver, London 1961

Hayward, J. F., *Huguenot Silver in England, 1688–1727*, London 1959

Honour, Hugh, *Goldsmiths and Silversmiths*, London 1971

Jackson, Sir Charles J., *The History of English Plate*, vols. I & II, London 1911

Oman, Charles, *Caroline Silver*, London 1970

Phillips, P. A. S., *Paul de Lamerie, His Life and Work*, London 1935

Rowe, Robert, *Adam Silver 1765–1795*, London 1965

INDEX

Page numbers set in **bold** type refer to illustrations

SOME OTHER TITLES IN THIS SERIES